All best wishes,
The ESQ

D1596282

converging lines

the extraordinary story of the emerson string quartet's first 25 years

by the emerson string quartet

Eugene Drucker

Lawrence Dutton

risk waters **group**

Published by the Risk Waters Group.

Haymarket House
28-29 Haymarket
London SW1Y 4RX
Tel: +44 (0)20 7484 9700
Fax: +44 (0)20 7484 9758

The Emerson String Quartet website is www.emersonquartet.com

ISBN 1 899332 68 5

British Library Cataloguing in Publication Data
A catalogue record for this book is available from the British Library

Printed and bound in the United Kingdom by dpi Print & Production, Tonbridge, Kent

Photograph on front cover by Andrew Eccles
Back cover illustration: doodles by Philip Setzer
Photographs on page 3 (opposite) by Christian Steiner (Philip & Linda Setzer, David Finckel & Wu Han,
Lawrence Dutton & Elizabeth Lim Dutton); Theodore Feibel (Eugene Drucker & Roberta Cooper); and
John Russell (Luke & Jesse Dutton)

The Emerson Quartet would like to thank
the following individuals and organizations whose assistance
and support made the creation of this book possible:

Peter Field, Risk Waters Group

Giles Smith, Risk Waters Group (Design)

Amy Bohr, Risk Waters Group (Design)

Danielle Leader, Risk Waters Group (Design)

Lloyd and Suzanne Joshel

Elizabeth Sobol, IMG Artists

Shirley Kirshbaum, Kirshbaum Demler & Associates, Inc.

Susan Demler, Kirshbaum Demler & Associates, Inc.

Ted and Yvonne Williams

Patrick Wood

Albrecht Ohly

Alexandra Ludwig

- and our families

contents

David Finckel
cello

Eugene Drucker
violin

Introduction

Philip Setzer
violin

Lawrence Dutton
viola

prologue

the story

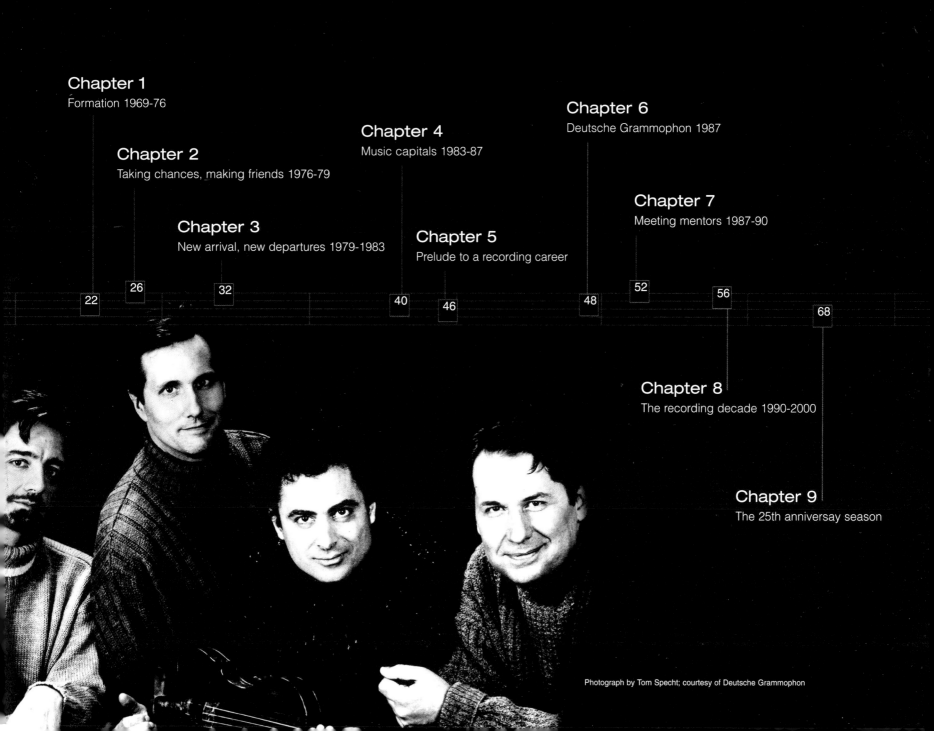

Introduction

When I first heard the Emerson Quartet in New York in 1987, I never dreamed that 14 years later I would end up helping them produce a book about themselves and having the privilege of writing the introduction for it.

As the book relates, that period since 1987 has been the Emerson's golden age. The Deutsche Grammophon contract was signed that year; the stream of major recordings started - Bartok, Beethoven and Shostakovich cycles, as well as other individual works; Grammy and Gramophone awards were won, and the group's reputation was definitively established.

And if their standing as recording artists became unparalleled, in their concert performances they moved into a class of their own. Anyone who went to the Shostakovich cycle in New York or London in 2000, or indeed anyone who witnessed their "Bartok Marathon" at the Queen Elizabeth Hall in London at the start of their 25th anniversary season in 2001 would testify to this. As Tom Service wrote in The Guardian (6 November 2001): "It would be difficult to imagine a more revelatory musical event, both in terms of Bartok's unique achievement and the Emersons' technical and interpretative mastery."

These last four words encapsulate the massive achievement of the quartet. Not only is it hard to think of another quartet which can play as faultlessly; it is equally hard to name one that so obviously thinks through every piece they perform as deeply. Which other quartet could appear to be effortlessly at home with Bartok one night, Haydn the next and Beethoven after that? Which tackles such a wide repertoire that also includes Schubert, Schumann and more modern music such Wolfgang Rihm, Edgar Meyer and Ned Rorem?

Even the configuration of the quartet is special, contributing to the freshness and vitality of the Emerson sound. The two violinists swap the leader's role between works or groups of works and the violist sits at the front right of the stage instead of the cello.

The text of the book takes the form of the four members of the quartet talking about their lives before and after the quartet and reminiscing about life on the road, in concert halls around the globe and in recording studios. They talk about their influences, their musical collaborators, the festivals and the friendships forged at them, their loved ones - everything that characterizes the Emerson extended family. Interspersed with the talk are historic pictures, programmes and reviews. Running through the chapters is a timeline, recording the history of the quartet in detail and highlighting the many "firsts" in its career.

The conversations the Emersons had about their lives together were recorded in September, 2001, in Wooster, Ohio and Berlin.

The crucial early years are given extended treatment. The book opens with a prologue in which the members of the quartet describe in turn how their lives came to converge on the Emerson. Then comes the story of how a hurried remark made by Eugene Drucker to Philip Setzer in 1970 sowed the seed of the Emerson's formation later on, with first Lawrence Dutton and then David Finckel joining. The early struggles and successes are described as the conversation leads on to the first major engagements, overseas tours and recordings. When

you come to the end of the astonishing chronicle of achievements, it's hard to believe all this was crammed into only 25 years.

Peter Field
Chairman & Chief Executive
Risk Waters Group Ltd

Prologue: the players

Philip Setzer
violin
Getting into music

My parents both played in the Cleveland Orchestra for many years - I grew up around the Cleveland Orchestra. At a very early age I heard classical music at home constantly, live and on the record player, and I started going to weekly concerts of the Orchestra under George Szell when the greatest soloists were coming through town regularly. So that kind of education is something you

can't really get in a school. It was a tremendous influence. At the age of four I went to my parents and said I wanted to play the violin. My parents said, "Well, you're too young. When you're five, if you still feel the same way then we can try it. The violin is not a toy - it's something that requires a real commitment." And so on my fifth birthday I walked into my parents bedroom in the morning and said, "I'm five years old. I want to play the violin." (They were still half asleep... "Go back to bed.") But they got me a violin. I started first with my father, who was a wonderful teacher - he taught a lot of young children at the Settlement Music School in Cleveland. Soon my father

felt that I had talent and that it would be better if I studied with someone else. So he talked to Josef Gingold, then concertmaster of the Cleveland Orchestra, and Gingold agreed to hear me. He took me as his student and I studied with him for almost three years. He was terrific - he had so much enthusiasm and I loved working with him. Unfortunately, at the age of 50, he decided to retire from the Orchestra and went to teach at Indiana University. I was about 9 years old, and when Rafael Druian came as the new concertmaster my parents talked to him on my behalf. I played for him and he took me as his student.

For the first few years when I was working with Druian, my mother would come to the lessons and then work with me at home. In a way she was sort of a translator - Druian was very intellectual and had never taught someone as young as I was - it was an experiment for him. During the lessons I could better understand what he was talking about, and my mother was very influential as his teaching assistant. It was she who really taught me how to practice. Druian took tremendous care with me, and worked with me diligently for almost eleven years - until I went to Juilliard. So he was in many ways my main teacher in learning to play the basics of the violin after Gingold and my father had given me a good start. Druian also taught me a lot about music - he was very demanding, but at the same time gave me self-confidence.

While in high school I still wasn't sure what I actually wanted to do - if I should go into music or go into medicine. And then I went to hear a concert of Oscar Shumsky, with whom my parents had studied at Peabody when they were twenty years old and he was twenty-three. The concert was at Oberlin - I remember the all-unaccompanied program of Telemann, Reger, Hindemith

Passacaglia for viola, and the Bach d-minor Partita. It was an unbelievable performance - there was a thunderstorm in the middle of the Chaconne and I thought: "Okay, okay, somebody's trying to tell me something. This is what I'm supposed to do with my life." I went backstage afterwards and asked if I could play for him. He accepted me as a student and I went to Juilliard and studied with him for 5 years. That's how I met Gene, who studied with him as well. Shumsky was a tremendous violinist and musician. I may have forgotten some of the things he told me, but I will never forget how monumental his playing was.

Introduction to chamber music

My father played in a quartet from the Cleveland Orchestra called the Symphonia Quartet - it was a very good goup and they often rehearsed at my house. When I was a kid I remember being told to go to bed and, sitting at the top of the steps, listening to them rehearse, talk, laugh and tell stories. It was the only time I really got to hear my father play other than his practicing at home. I loved the sound of the quartet - just hearing the enjoyment they had. I remember hearing some arguments too - and how interesting it was the way they resolved things and went on. But that was a very big influence that has stayed with me, the sound of the string quartet from the top of the stairs. Also, listening to the Budapest Quartet Beethoven recordings, and the Schubert Cello Quintet: Those are the pieces I remember listening to most, as they were always on, always being played.

The summer before I attended Juilliard, I had my first real chamber music experience at the Blossom School at Kent State University. I played the Brahms C-minor Piano Quartet, and the feeling in that performance was something that changed my whole sense of what I might want to do. I remember walking in the parking lot afterwards with my mother and saying to her, "You know, there's something really amazing about being up there with a few other people. I never

The Busch Quartet, with Ernst Drucker, far right

Elmer Setzer, middle, with the Symphonia Quartet and Glenn Gould. The quartet premiered Gould's one-movement string quartet and performed the Shostakovich Quintet with him for a television broadcast.

really felt anything like that. I think that's what I might want to do." There are occasions when your life takes a turn, and you're not really aware of it at the time because you have so many options open to you. But when you look back, you realize that these were real pivotal moments.

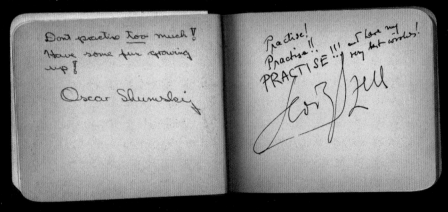

Don't practice too much! Have some fun growing up!

Oscar Shumsky

Practise! Practise!! PRACTISE!!! and have my very best wishes!

George Szell

There's a social issue here, which brings to mind a story: As a teenager, I played a concerto with an amateur orchestra in Cleveland. George Szell came to listen to a rehearsal. After several minutes, he went to my father and said' "He's got talent. He really could have a career as a soloist, but he'd have to be taken out of school, he'd have to be tutored, practice ten hours a day." My father said, "Well, thank you very much...but I think I know how I want to raise my son." And they actually had a fight. I'm there playing the Bruch concerto, looking out seeing Szell and my father in the back of Severance Hall arguing, and then Szell stalking out. On another occasion I went backstage to get Szell's autograph (I had quite a collection of autographs from 1960-1962) and Szell wrote in my book, "Practise! Practise!! PRACTISE!!! And have my very best wishes, George Szell". The next year Oscar Shumsky came to Cleveland to play, and I went and asked for his autograph, and he started looking through my book to see who else was in there. And he came upon the autograph from Szell and read it, and kind of snickered a little bit, and on the opposite page he wrote, "Don't practice too much, have some fun growing up. Oscar Shumsky". So I've got these in my book facing each other. But what I want to say is that there were elements in my life that led to my wanting to be in a string quartet rather than pursuing a solo career - and I really found that this was right for me. I'm not saying that ignoring what Szell said led me to being a string quartet player - as if by not working hard enough, I ended up playing in a quartet - but I didn't want that kind of life for myself. I didn't want to be removed from school, from my friends - I wanted to be in a social situation. To make the kind of music that we make in a quartet, to play the repertoire that we have, and also to have that social interaction, is extremely gratifying to me. Of course sometimes it's difficult, but that's really the way I want to live my life rather than sit around alone and practice ten hours a day.

I also went to the Marlboro Music Festival in the mid-70's. The way that Marlboro works is that there is a senior member in each group who leads the rehearsals from within the group - I had the experience of playing first violin in Haydn's "Lark" Quartet with Alexander Schneider (the former second violinist of the Budapest String Quartet) playing second violin. This was an amazing experience along the road to forming my own quartet.

Eugene Drucker
violin
Getting into music

My father was a violinist. He played with the Busch Quartet at the end of World War II for a couple of years (Adolf Busch, the first violinist of the quartet, had been my father's idol when my father was studying in Germany). He immigrated to the US in 1938 and was in a variety of orchestras for the next few years: the NBC Symphony, one season with the Cleveland Orchestra under Rodzinski, and then with the Busch Chamber Players while he was in the quartet, after he was discharged from the Army.

After a few years with the Quartet, he felt that the touring life (my older brother just having been born) was too much of a strain on the family, so he auditioned for the Metropolitan Opera Orchestra where Adolf Busch's brother Fritz was the principal conductor. I think he didn't realize in 1947 that he would be at the Met for the next 38 years, until his retirement. Chamber music and solo violin music, as well as orchestra playing, were a very strong part of his experience. But one difference between Phil 's childhood and mine is that I was not so directly involved with my father's functioning in the orchestra from week to week. I didn't hear all of his performances because it was not so easy to go to the Met - they had seven performances a week, and he was away a great deal of the time. In those days the musicians didn't get many performances off - I think it was one night every three weeks. Operas are much longer than normal concerts - so as a child I didn't go to too many of them. But we did go to summer festivals: Chautauqua (in western New York State) where my father played in the symphony orchestra and was concertmaster of the opera. I went there for 11 summers, from the age of six (which was before I started playing an instrument) until I was 17. There I heard a lot of the symphonic repertoire, and although the orchestra was not quite on the level of the Cleveland Orchestra, they had a lot of members of the Pittsburgh Symphony and many other fine players from throughout the USA. I became fascinated watching all of the different instruments being played and somehow associating the characteristics of the players with the instruments themselves. I also heard a lot of operas. In Chautauqua they did all of the operas in English, but at least I got a certain grounding.

I started playing violin at the age of 8, partly because the first two summers at Chautauqua I went to day camp and had a miserable experience the second summer. I almost got thrown out. The third summer I refused to go to the Boys Club, as it was called, and I had to find something else to do with my time. I took an art class for about a week. There were people in my family that had a great deal of visual artistic talent, but I was pathetic at it - I couldn't do anything. That avenue was clearly closed to me, and the only thing left besides doing well at school was to start playing an instrument. I had studied the piano briefly when I was about 5 years old, but I didn't stick with it. So at the age of 8 I had to re-learn to read notes, and started the violin. After my father had taught me for about four months, he had to go on tour with the Met - which they did every spring for about 7 or 8 weeks - and he realized that since I had only been playing for four months, it was crucial to find a teacher for me.

It happened that in our neighborhood, in Washington Heights, there was a little conservatory just a few blocks away, where a colleague of my father's from Chautauqua was teaching. Her name was Reneé Hurtig, but her maiden name was Galimir, and she was the older sister of the well-known violinist Felix Galimir. She had been the violist of the original Galimir Quartet, which was active in Vienna as a champion of contemporary music (which at that time even included the Ravel Quartet!) and they also played Berg's Lyric Suite and quartets by Schoenberg and Webern, before emigrating to the United States. Reneé Hurtig was struggling to make a living freelancing in New York, and had to make a huge commute from where she lived on 74th street and 1st Avenue all the way up to the conservatory in Washington Heights. I worked with her from the age of 9, and by the time I was 13 Reneé decided it was time for me to go to somebody else - an "artist teacher", as she called it. She wanted me to study with Erica Morini because she had grown up in Vienna idolizing Morini. So I played an audition in November of 1965 in her 5th Avenue apartment. I was somewhat nervous, and she didn't accept me as a student. In retrospect I'm very grateful for this, because two months later I auditioned for Oscar Shumsky, who did accept me. I became his youngest student at 13 - his only

student in the Juilliard Preparatory division. He was a tremendous musical influence on me as I expanded and refined my violin technique and learned to deepen my approach to great works of music in various styles. He had tremendous integrity, which was always an example to me. I studied with him for the next 7 years. I did have other musical influences, too; I was going to the High School of Music and Art and had a composition teacher, a wonderful man who gave me a very good grounding in theory and encouraged me in some early student compositions.

At the age of 16 I was able to go to the Tanglewood Music Festival, where I met violinist Joseph Silverstein, then concertmaster of the Boston Symphony Orchestra. He was very encouraging to me in terms of my future possibilities. He said that there was something about me that reminded him of himself twenty years earlier, and he encouraged me to do international competitions - something Shumsky was not interested in at all. Shumsky gave me an ideal sense of what it was like to be a musician, to be immersed in a score, to be well-rounded. He later encouraged my studies at Columbia as well as Juilliard. But he deplored the trends in the music world - he was not interested in violin competitions and did not give me any concrete guidance on how to build a career, so that aspect of my development had to be encouraged by someone else. Silverstein, like Shumsky, was a conductor. I remember playing Berlioz's Harold in Italy at Tanglewood when Silverstein did some of his early conducting. The violin sectional rehearsals that Silverstein conducted were fascinating. I learned a great deal about how to play in an orchestra from him, which proved valuable when I later became concertmaster of the Juilliard Orchestra.

At Tanglewood I also met Gunther Schuller, who was a big influence, and got very involved with contemporary music there. The main thing I remember about Tanglewood was that there were three main categories of activity: orchestra, chamber music and contemporary music. We rehearsed about nine hours a day; each category would get rehearsed three hours a day and I loved it. I can't imagine that now, loving to rehearse nine hours a day, but at that point my enthusiasm and idealism were at a peak and I was amazed by all these different influences I was getting.

Introduction to chamber music

When I was finished with high school I went to Columbia, where I majored in English and Comparative Literature, and I also went to Juilliard, where I was coached in chamber music by Felix Galimir and members of the Juilliard Quartet. It was in my third year of Juilliard that an embryonic form of what was to become the ESQ started.

After Tanglewood, the next major festival I attended was Marlboro, where I spent five summers from the ages of 20 to 24. I learned many string quartets there which I would later play with the Emerson. I worked on a lot of music from the second Viennese school, because Felix Galimir played a major role at Marlboro. I also had the privilege of playing a quintet with Rudolf Serkin, and in the Marlboro Festival Orchestra under Pablo Casals. There was a multitude of influences that were important to me. The flexibility that is required for quartet-playing is tested in all the ad hoc ensembles that you play with in a festival like Marlboro. You always encounter certain dominating personalities, maybe some recessive personalities, and frequent instances of different instrumental styles because the players come from all over the world. You have to attempt to produce a cohesive product, at least temporarily. So I would say that Marlboro was a very important factor in my early life as a musician.

Lawrence Dutton
viola
Getting into music

My background couldn't be more different from Gene's and Phil's. I started music in the public school system of suburban New York, on Long Island, in Wantagh. There was a very special man there, named Eugene Kahn, who ran the string program and was a violinist. I remember playing the tonette (which is a plastic recorder) in the third grade and enjoying that a lot. They brought us all down at the end of the year,

the third graders, to hear the orchestra and band concerts, and I heard the orchestra play and loved the string sound. So we were invited to come after school and see the instruments, and I remember the first instrument brought in was the violin and I never went any further. When I got home I told my parents that I wanted to play the violin. I started with group lessons and after about a year Mr. Kahn came to my mother and said I needed private lessons, that I had talent - so he would come to my house and work with me privately. He took me to the various NY State Music Association Competitions and the little orchestra things, the County and the New York State orchestras.

Ivan Galamian, the great violin pedagogue, had three assistants: Dorothy Delay, Sally Thomas, and Margaret Pardee. Mr. Kahn knew Margaret Pardee, arranged an audition for me, and I started studying with her. So Kahn was really the one responsible for putting me on the right track. I worked with Miss Pardee from seventh grade through high school and by eleventh grade I was going to the Juilliard School pre-college division. During my last year of pre-college she had me start playing some viola and I found an instrument with a voice that I loved, and which was a comfortable size for me. So Miss Pardee was largely responsible for my becoming a violist. Coming from a situation where I was one of a pack of violinists, I suddenly found myself as principal viola of the Juilliard pre-college orchestra and Long Island Youth

Orchestra, and thought "this is pretty good!" I was also studying chamber music at Juilliard pre-college and got the chance to play with some extraordinary young string players that included a fine violinist, Sung Ju Lee, and a young Chinese cellist named Yo-Yo Ma. Due to my family's financial situation, however, I wasn't able to attend Juilliard School immediately out of high school. Juilliard had offered a good scholarship, but Eastman came up with an extraordinary scholarship and I decided to go there.

When I went to Eastman I had a wonderful teacher named Francis Tursi, who was very important for me. In my second year I was into all kinds of things at the school - a little electric violin and viola, a little jazz fusion - and eventually Tursi said, "Well, Larry, when are you going to get serious about playing the viola?" And then I realized that I should go back to New York.

I feel I was fortunate to have gone to a public school with a good music program. Coming from a non-musical background, there would have been no other way for me but public education, and I owe a lot to Eugene Kahn, who was smart and unselfish enough to give up one of his prize pupils. Without his guidance, my parents wouldn't have known that Miss Pardee was the right choice. The most important thing is not that all students in public education become concert artists, but that they develop a love for music and become the future audiences so that we have people who understand what the great things are of our civilization. It enhances the quality of life.

Introduction to chamber music

When I started to work with Miss Pardee, my family couldn't afford to send me to Meadowmount, Galamian's summer music camp. There was one music camp called Star Lake in upstate New York and I went there for two weeks when I was 13. The Lenox String Quartet was in residence there, as well as violinist and pedagogue Samuel Applebaum (the father of

Guarneri Quartet violist Michael Tree), so I played my first chamber music under Michael Tree's father, which seems incredible to me now. Plus, there were some very good students there. So in this way I was exposed to chamber music for the first time. My first piece was the Haydn "Lark" Quartet, and I played 1st violin. I thought "Wow, this is one of the most amazing things." Later, in high school, I met another student of Miss Pardee, Lenny Rivlin. His Dad was a great record collector and had all the old Budapest and Smetana Quartet recordings. We listened to this stuff constantly and it was an incredible learning experience.

When I returned to Juilliard after Eastman, Robert Mann of the Juilliard Quartet was very supportive to me, a very important influence. I also coached with Felix Galimir, and Juilliard Quartet members Joel Krosnick and Sam Rhodes, who became a really great mentor to me. He also sold me my first really good viola - it was an Otto Erdesz. I used that instrument my first seven years in the ESQ. Also, he lent me an old Italian instrument that I used on some of the early ESQ recordings. I was fortunate to participate in Alexander Schneider's Christmas String Seminar at Carnegie Hall, where I met all kinds of musicians. My teacher, Lillian Fuchs, a terrific violist, also played in a string quartet that had performed every week on WQXR radio for 23 years. She was an important influence and a direct connection to the great older traditions of string playing.

In New York I also found people that loved chamber music - there was sort of a club of us. I started hanging out with violinist Daniel Phillips (now of the Orion Quartet) and violist Ira Weller, (now in the Metropolitan Opera Orchestra). They had an apartment that was very soundproof and you could read chamber music all through the night without bothering anybody. We would read through everything - we read most of the Haydn Quartets over a period of years - all kinds of terrific musicians would show up and play. In the last year of school I became Samuel Rhodes' teaching assistant, and I got to know all of the chamber music students and faculty. I became very good friends with Nicky Mann (the son of Robert Mann and violinist of the Mendelssohn Quartet) and we played quartets together.

During this time I occasionally played in the Orpheus Chamber Orchestra, and it was while working with that group that Phil and I met at a recording gig. He invited me to audition for the Emerson Quartet, but at the same time I was offered the position of solo violist of the Stuttgart Chamber Orchestra, and they invited me to start the following season. I had been studying with Lillian Fuchs, and I showed her the letter. She said "No, you can't. You have to stay and continue studying." So she made me write to them saying I couldn't take the job. At the same time, I had also taken an audition with the rock band Emerson, Lake and Palmer. They were going on a gigantic 5-month world tour, with an orchestra. I got the position and I accepted it. So I also had to tell them I couldn't do it. I had to go to the Musician's Union and write a letter of apology, since I had made a verbal agreement. It was my first lesson in the music business. Fortunately, I hadn't taken any of those positions - they would have prevented me from meeting Phil and eventually joining the ESQ. I think it's interesting that my early career was a combination of the mentoring process, luck and networking (that word didn't exist then!), finding the right people, and making the right connections.

David Finckel
cello
Getting into music

I was born into a musical family. It was like being born into a family that runs a farm or a business - my parents had started a music camp when I was a kid and my father gave music lessons in the house. I learned to play an instrument and started teaching like my father. I didn't know how to do anything else and never really considered that I would - never for a moment did I think that I would be anything but a musician for my entire life. And that was fine with me because everyone around me seemed to be having a great time - it was a great community, there were people in the household studying and my mother was in the kitchen cooking, and my father was teaching, and I was teaching. We worked together to build a music camp in Vermont when I was about 10 or 11 years old - which was about the time I started playing the cello.

My father was my first teacher. He taught me how to think, how to concentrate, and later I also had a pretty tough cello teacher, Mary Gili, who made the same demands on me when I was just beginning. The school where my father taught for almost 40 years, called the Far Brook School, is a very progressive school where children are exposed to great works of art from an early age: plays of Shakespeare, music of Bach and Handel. My father fell right into that philosophy because he always believed that children should be given the best of the arts, that nothing should be dumbed-down and that a child's capacity to understand and even perform great works was practically limitless. So I had my sights set very high artistically when I was a kid - I was not ever made aware of limitations in music or the music business. Actually, my parents didn't know much about the music business - they didn't care. They never did anything for money - just out of love and dedication to their ideals. It was a long time before I learned how to do things like write a check, and lead a responsible life - at least responsible to other people. But I was lucky because I got my fingers into the cello and liked it, and after a couple of years, after I learned to make a vibrato, things really clicked. Because I had listened to good records since I was a kid it bothered me tremendously that I couldn't make the same sounds I heard on the records. But as soon as my vibrato kicked in I thought, "Wow, I can sound good!" and I really took off and started practicing a lot. Before it was just agony - like any other kid trying to learn an instrument.

Not long after that my cellist uncle George (there are a lot a cellists in my family) called up my father one day and said, "Go out and get a record by this cellist, write down the name, I'll spell it for you: R-O-S-T-R-O-P-O-V-I-C-H." So we went out and found a record, and it was like I had been shot through by an arrow. Rostropovich's sound and intensity, his technique and musicianship, it was like, where has this sound been? It was as though I was hearing a sound that had been inside me from the beginning but had never before become external. Right then I decided that I wanted to learn to play the cello from this guy, but how? I went on to pursue him during his early tours in the United States and eventually got the courage to ask to play for him. He very graciously gave me lessons for a number of years, whenever I could manage to get near where he was. I never did go to Moscow to study with him, which I probably should have done, but it was impossible. I was still a kid in school, but my parents would get me out of school if I said "Rostropovich is playing in Boston, I want to take the bus up there". They were very progressive in their thinking. So I chased Rostropovich around like a dog following a bone, and got tons of inspiration just being around him. I was also absorbed in his process of new music commissioning. Every couple years when he'd come for a tour he'd have a new concerto by Shostakovich or Benjamin Britten. I'd get the music and learn it, and study it with him and through him get this feeling of connection to the composer. He's been the first performer of over 100 new works at this point in his life - the most significant contribution to the literature of any instrument by any performer. It was an incredibly exciting time, and I worked very, very hard.

I went to college for only one year - I wanted a much more rigorous experience than I was offered there - and besides, I had the opportunity to

study with Rostropovich when I could get to him and having to go to school was just a distraction from that. (Although I did have the opportunity to study with Bernard Greenhouse for a year, and he was a very positive influence and very encouraging.) I should also mention that Elsa Hilger, a phenomenal cellist from the Philadelphia Orchestra, was a teacher who also encouraged me from the age of 13. I was a pretty shy kid, and she was not at all shy, and talked to me endlessly about how she loved to perform, and somehow I was impressionable

enough at that age to believe I could love it too. She helped me work up my nerve to go out on stage and do what I loved in public. I entered more competitions and got to play with the Philadelphia Orchestra twice, as winner of the orchestra's junior and senior student competitions.

Introduction to chamber music

My early experiences in ensemble playing were limited to orchestra and chamber orchestra. My father conducted a chamber orchestra in New Jersey, and I used to organize the chamber groups at our music camp, Point Counterpoint. I had limited chamber music experience - I never performed a quartet except for perhaps once, before the ESQ came along. My musical life was mostly involved with solo cello repertoire and orchestral repertoire - I can practically play the Brandenburg Concerti by heart - and I learned all the solo literature which I now put to good use. And then I spent some seasons as one of two cellists of the Concerto Soloists of Philadelphia, which was (and still is) a very high-quality ensemble, which satisfied me. Eventually I made the move to New York City, which people told me was important: if I wanted to connect to important musicians I should eat at such-and-such Chinese restaurant, I should be seen here and there, otherwise people wouldn't know that I was interested in working. So I got an apartment on 98th street and started to freelance. Some of the first musical work I did involved some of the other members of the ESQ and that's how I got to know the other guys.

Photograph by Werner Neumeister; courtesy of Deutsche Grammophon

Chapter 1

Formation 1969-76

A casual idea becomes history

PS: Gene and I met and became friends as students of Oscar Shumsky in 1969. Shumsky had an open class once a month for all of his students, and we admired each other's playing. Also, that year we had both been assigned to student quartets. But at the end of the first year, we mentioned to each other that neither of our quartets was working out. The very last day of school I had some library books to return. I was in a hurry and as I ran in I heard Gene call me: "I want to ask you something. This will just take a second. I was wondering if you would like to be in a quartet with me next year?" And I said "Oh yeah, sure." "We could form a quartet rather than being assigned to one. I have some ideas about people we could work with." "Sounds good to me. Definitely, let's do it. I really have to run now." As the door was closing, Gene called to me and said "We'll switch on the violin parts, okay?" And I said "Sure, fine." Looking back on it, that was the moment when the Quartet really started, in the Spring of 1970.

Personnel upheavals

We talked over the summer and decided who the other members would be. And right from the beginning we had problems (not between Gene and me!). The original cellist, Larry Dreyfus, was a excellent player; I remember we had a rehearsal on a Saturday at his place, and were supposed to rehearse again on Sunday. We finished rehearsing and I left my music stand and music there because we were going to rehearse the next morning. I went out on a date that night, and when I came back there was a bag in front of my apartment door. In it was my music and music stand and a note from Larry Dreyfus saying, "I know this is kind of sudden, but I've decided to go to rabbinical school. And I'm not pursuing music at this time." So, between 2pm and 10pm that Saturday, he'd made this monumental decision to change the course of his life (he's now back playing music again).

Our original violist was Marna Street, who later became principal violist in the Cincinnati Symphony. She graduated not long after we got together, and decided not to stay in the quartet.

ED: The first piece we tried to play was the "Harp" Quartet of Beethoven. We gave up on it because it was too difficult and moved on to the Bartok 2nd. It took us the whole year to learn one piece. We had a couple of different cellists after Larry Dreyfus left: the first was Fred Zlotkin, and then Eric Wilson, a student of Leonard Rose, for the second semester. He was the cellist with the ESQ from then until David arrived.

PS: In the fall of 1971 Guillermo Figueroa became our violist. He and I had played together during the summer in Vermont, with the Craftsbury Chamber Players. We then worked together in the quartet for a few years while we were at Juilliard. By the time we graduated in 1974, we had performed three pieces: Bartok 2nd, Bartok 4th, and Beethoven Op.132. We were functioning very sporadically at that point, and did not yet have the name Emerson String Quartet.

Making a living

ED:I finished school early and played one season, about 20 or 25 concerts, with a very fine modern music group called Speculum Musicae, where I got a lot of good experience. In addition, I was starting to freelance, and I joined the New York Chamber Soloists, whose director Melvin Kaplan was a not only an oboist but a contractor and manager as well. I played with some orchestras, such as the Musica Aeterna, and also the Brandenburg Ensemble - which was a kind of offshoot of the Marlboro Festival. Alexander Schneider was the conductor and was a big influence on many young musicians at that time.

PS: We were all freelancing - playing in the Brooklyn Philharmonia, Westchester Philharmonic...

ED: Another group we were in actually had David Finckel in the cello section. It was called the Empire Sinfonietta and lasted only a few years. We worked with several distinguished conductors, among them Rafael Druian and Aaron Copland, who conducted us for some television programs. Shumsky conducted as well, and brought David with him from his orchestra in New Jersey. When David joined the quartet years later I didn't realize it was the same person - he had grown a beard in the meantime, and his face looked so different that my memory was jogged only when I saw a picture of him from his late teens, and I said, "Wait a second, didn't you play...?"

DF: I was a quiet, shy New Jersey boy trying to interact with seemingly very intimidating, high-powered New York musicians.

Competitions, decisions

PS: Between 1974 and 76, Gene and I entered solo competitions, while keeping the quartet on the back burner (playing occasional concerts in churches, and sometimes at weddings and funerals). We hadn't yet made the commitment to a career as a quartet. We went together to the Sibelius Competition in Helsinki, and both did pretty badly. Then we went to the Queen Elisabeth Competition in Brussels in 1976 and did very well, both making the finals. Yet we didn't win one of the very top prizes, and I remember on the bus to the airport saying, "Well, I think that's it for competitions. What about the quartet? Should we really look at that?" And right there on that bus we made the decision to talk to the other guys when we got back.

We had had a lot of encouragement from others as well. The Juilliard Quartet had a tremendous influence on us, especially early on, while we were students. We had some coachings with Claus Adam, the Juilliard cellist, but our main quartet coach over those years was their first violinist Robert Mann. He was a great teacher - always inspiring, demanding and encouraging. Our relationship continued with him after we graduated because he was the president of the Naumburg Competition, which we won in 1978. Bobby has remained a great supporter and friend of our quartet over the years.

We had played some concerts in churches, as I mentioned earlier, and Peter Mennin, then president of the Juilliard School came to one of them. He later invited us into his office and asked, "Have you thought about making a go of it as a quartet? I really think you have the potential to do it." We knew that there must be something special about the quartet - we just needed to get all the other stuff out of the way first. ◖

▽ Eugene and Philip amongst the other winners at the 1976 Queen Elisabeth Competition

Chapter 2

Taking chances, making friends 1976-79

Management

PS: In 1976 we decided to go for it. Melvin Kaplan, the contractor-manager, knew that there was a quartet out there that Gene was involved with. He asked Gene at one point what was happening with the quartet. And when we decided to really commit to it seriously, Mel took a chance and offered us management.

He had never heard us. Gene deserves a lot of credit because Mel thought that anything Gene was involved with had to be on a high level!

ED: Mel told us he was going to stick his neck out and book 20 concerts for us the following season with presenters that he knew. In addition, he invited us to come play at the Vermont Mozart Festival, which he directed. We needed to learn about a dozen quartets for that summer.

We also needed to quickly come up with a name for the group. 1976 was the American Bicentennial year, so we chose the name Emerson (after the philosopher Ralph Waldo Emerson). We wanted to have an American name with cultural associations. By the way, how we chose the name is our most frequently asked question!

A first try at the Naumburg Competition

PS. Right from the beginning, we decided to work toward the 1977 Naumburg Competition. There were some problems within the group, specifically with Guillermo, because he was not sure how much "viola time" he could commit to (he was really a terrific violinist, and also a Shumsky student). Guillermo decided a couple of weeks before the competition that it just wasn't going to be right - what if we won and then he left the group? It would have been very messy. So after we had already passed the tape round we went to Robert Mann, who was head of the competition, and said, "This is the situation, we think we should withdraw." It was the right thing to do, and he respected our decision. We really had no idea who would replace Guillermo.

ED: At the same time, the quartet had committed itself to a project funded by the Rockefeller Foundation: New World Records was recording 100 LP's which would present a historical overview of American music. We eventually made two recordings for that series. Elizabeth Ostrow, who later produced for us for

Deutsche Grammophon, was the producer of these first recordings of our career. We made the first one with Masao Kawasaki as temporary violist. He's a fine violinist and violist, and in addition has become a very prominent teacher.

Finding the right violist

PS: We began trying out violists. We auditioned a total of 11, and Larry Dutton was one of them.

LD: At that point I had only one year of Juilliard left to go, and I had become increasingly interested in playing chamber music. I was freelancing and meeting people who were involved in chamber music and who were in the Orpheus Chamber Orchestra. I had gone on some Orpheus tours, and had met Guillermo, and Jerry Grossman, who is now one of the principal cellists of the Metropolitan Opera Orchestra. Jerry and I had read chamber music together, and he was good friends with Phil. I was playing a recording session for Orpheus, and Jerry Grossman knew the ESQ was looking for a violist. I had heard about the Emerson - they were famous already among the Juilliard crowd - and I thought "Wow, an amazing group." I know from my date book that I first met Phil in May 1977, at an Orpheus rehearsal. Both he and Guillermo were original members of that group.

PS: So Jerry said to me, "Hey, you should play with this guy." I'd seen him, but didn't really know him. So Jerry introduced us, and we talked a bit and I invited Larry to audition.

ED: Melvin Kaplan invited us to the Vermont Mozart Festival that summer.

1976-77 First Season

September	**Emerson String Quartet** formed at the Juilliard School, NY, from previously active student ensemble. **Philip Setzer, Eugene Drucker**, violins; **Guillermo Figueroa**, viola; **Eric Wilson**, cello
November	Quartet is signed by **Melvin Kaplan, Inc.,** NY
March	First professional concerts in the **Cleveland, Ohio** area
April	Guillermo Figueroa leaves quartet
May	The quartet's **first recording,** for New World Records, with Masao Kawasaki playing viola. Works by Roy Harris, Arthur Shepherd and Henry Cowell
June	Lawrence Dutton joins quartet as violist
July	First appearances at the **Vermont Mozart Festival,** Burlington, **Vermont**

1977-78 Second Season

September	**Englewood, New Jersey**
October	First tour: four concerts, in **Corpus Christi, Texas, Oak Ridge, Tennessee, Mobile, Alabama,** and **Santa Fe, New Mexico**
January	**Worchester, Massachusetts**
February	Piston Concerto for String Quartet, Wind Instruments and Percussion in first appearance at **Carnegie Hall, NY**
	Second recording for New World Records, with Lawrence Dutton playing viola
	Works by Andrew Imbrie and Gunther Schuller
	Pierpont Morgan Library, NY
	Mt. Holyoke, Massachussetts
March	**Library of Congress,** Washington, DC
	Cincinnati, Ohio
April	Quartet wins **Naumburg Award for Chamber Music**
May	Recording of the **Piston Concerto,** for the CRI label. With the Juilliard Orchestra, Sixten Ehrling, conductor
July	First concerts with Beaux Arts Trio pianist **Menahem Pressler,** at the Vermont Mozart Festival
July	First concert in **Boston,** at Massachusetts Institute of Technology
August	First appearance at the **Caramoor Festival,** New York

The festival not only offered us performance experience but also gave us a place to be together, to work together, to get to know each other socially as well as professionally. It was a very important opportunity for us to find ourselves.

PS: Larry worked with us during the summer of 1977 and that was really the solidifying experience. It was not an invitation to definitely join, but simply to try it out to see if it worked for everyone. It was not easy. We had to rehearse long hours in order to learn a huge amount of repertoire, and we didn't know each other very well. It was a several-week-long audition - which is not exactly the most relaxing way to spend a summer. Larry didn't have a lot of experience, and neither did we, for that matter, but it became clear as the summer went on that the group sounded better and better. We also connected personally and had a lot of fun, and felt by the end of the summer that it was going to work. Eric, Gene and I made a commitment to Larry and Larry accepted. So there we have 3/4 of the now-existing Emerson Quartet.

LD: I was finishing my Bachelor's and knew that I was going to get my Master's the next year. So during my first year in the ESQ I was still at Juilliard, but we didn't have that many concerts. I was a little younger - when I joined the ESQ I had just turned 23 - and I suddenly had to learn all of these masterpieces. But that was what I wanted to do, so I pushed myself really hard.

The most difficult adjustment I had to make was simply to catch up. Gene and Phil were already out of Juilliard and were working on professional careers, while I was still at school, feeling like a student. However, the Emerson wasn't like some other groups, for example the Guarneri Quartet, who when they started had a major career quickly, with something like 100 concerts per season. For me it was just right because we only had about 20 concerts that first season. We rehearsed a lot and worked very hard.

First Season, first tour

PS: After that summer each of us was still doing a lot of freelancing. Larry was still in school. So there was much juggling of schedules and rehearsing between other commitments. It was a scramble to try and find the time to work together, but we all were committed to doing it. And we did play 20 concerts that season - made a ton of money - probably each of us came away with a few thousand dollars.

In October 1977 we went on our first official tour. There were four concerts: Corpus Christi, Texas; Oak Ridge, Tennessee; Mobile, Alabama; and Santa Fe, New Mexico. In Santa Fe we made an extra $500 teaching. When we came home each of us had cleared $50, after expenses. But we made money! We were a professional quartet, we came out ahead!

The Naumburg, again

ED: In the spring of 1978 we finally entered and won the Naumburg Competition for Chamber Music, which gave us, as a goal to work towards, a debut recital at Lincoln Center a year later. And that was the first springboard - the first big event in the career of the Quartet where we felt something propelling us forward. A second Naumburg concert was planned for the following season, in which we we'd premiere the work that was being written for us as part of the Naumburg prize - Mario Davidovsky's 4th String Quartet.

An early Carnegie Hall appearance

PS: In February 1978 we were asked to play Walter Piston's Concerto for String Quartet with the National Orchestra Association at Carnegie Hall. It was good exposure for the quartet, and we later recorded the piece with the Juilliard Orchestra for CRI.

The Smithsonian Institution

ED: In November 1978 we began a relationship with the Smithsonian Institution in Washington, DC, which continues to this day. We were invited by Anthony Ames and Christopher Kendall, members of a group known as the 20th Century Consort, to participate in some of their concerts at the Hirshhorn Museum. It was in one of those concerts that we played our first performance of the Bartok 5th, and also Gunther Schuller's 2nd Quartet, which we later recorded for New World Records, along with Andrew Imbrie's 4th Quartet.

The director of the National Endowment for the Arts came to one of those early Smithsonian concerts and encouraged us to apply for a grant. We were later fortunate to receive three grants from the NEA which helped us immensely in our early years - they enabled us to keep functioning until the point where we were able to survive exclusively on quartet engagements. It was a full five years, up to about 1982, before we began making a living from playing quartets.

1978-79 Third Season

October	**Glen Cove, Long Island, NY**
November	First appearance on radio station WQXR's **"The Listening Room"**, Robert Sherman, host
	First concerts at the **Smithsonian Institution**, Washington, DC
	Tour: **Akron, Ohio, University of Arkansas, Fayetteville, Arkansas; Vanderbilt University, Nashville**, Tennessee
December	First appearance at the **Metropolitan Museum of Art, NY**
January	Tour: **Indiana University, Bloomington, Indiana; University of California, Los Angeles, California; University of California, Berkeley, California; Cleveland, Ohio**
	Tour: **Eugene, Oregon; Santa Fe, New Mexico; Allentown, Pennsylvania; Kansas City, Missouri**
February	**Vermont Mozart Festival Winter Series; Rhode Island Chamber Music Concerts, Providence, Rhode Island; Charleston Chamber Music Society, Charleston, West Virginia; Romantic Chamber Ensemble**, Smithsonian Institution, Washington, DC
March	**Lincoln Center debut at Alice Tully Hall** as Naumburg Award-winners
	Chappaqua, NY; Princeton, New Jersey; **Wilton**, Connecticut
	First appearance at the **Kennedy Center**, Washington, DC
April	**YM-YWHA of Washington Heights, NY; Sherman, Texas**
July	**Vermont Mozart Festival**
August 16	**Newport Opera Festival**, Newport, Rhode Island
	Last concert with Eric Wilson

LD: There was another group at the Smithsonian called the Romantic Chamber Ensemble, many of whose members also played in the 20th Century Consort. They performed at a different venue, the beautiful Renwick Gallery on Pennsylvania Avenue. We appeared on some of their programs as well and this led to our first series, partially funded by the National Endowment for the Arts, which began in the fall of '79, when David Finckel had just joined us. Our associations with these two high-quality groups, supported enthusiastically by the Smithsonian, somehow evolved rather quickly into an Emerson and Friends series, and later, after the series was adopted by the Smithsonian's Resident Associates division, it became the Emerson Quartet series at the Baird Auditorium in the Natural History Museum. This annual series of four or five concerts per season, played for an extremely discerning audience, remains one of the mainstays of our often-hectic concert life.

The New York debut, and a farewell to Eric

PS: In March 1979, for our Naumburg debut at Lincoln Center's Alice Tully Hall, we played three quartets: the Mozart "Dissonance", Smetana and Bartok 5. We received a very good review from the NY Times, but soon afterwards Eric Wilson decided to leave the Quartet. He wanted to take a teaching position at the University of British Columbia in Vancouver. So we played our last summer with Eric, ending our quartet partnership with a concert at the Newport Opera Festival. I remember playing the Barber Adagio on the program, and it was very sad. We parted with Eric on the best of terms and have remained close friends. He has joined us a number of times since, as guest cellist in the Schubert Quintet. o

7/18/77 Burlington Free Press

Opening Night of Mozart Festival Brings Memories, Superb Program

◁ Earliest review, from the Vermont Mozart Festival, 1977

By JOHN D. DONOGHUE
Free Press Music Critic

The fourth Vermont Festival opened Sunday evening with a full house — make that a full barn — some superlative Mozart, Haydn and Vivaldi, plus rain.

For a short time the rain on the roof of the University of Vermont's Show Barn reminded this listener of the night under a tent at Tanglewood when Koussevitzky stormed off stage, raging at the damp counterpoint that drummed the "Rienzi" Overture into silence. He returned, launched into the "Ride of the Valkyries" and resolved to build a permanent shell.

Actually, the Show Barn has marvelous acoustics for chamber music and for the Vivaldi choruses. It not only reflects the sound cleanly, but also with warmth.

The New York Chamber Soloists are back and with them came Julius Baker, soloist in the Mozart Concerto in D major for flute, strings, oboes and French horns, K.314.

New to us was the Emerson String Quartet which also battled the elements briefly before triumphing with the Quartet in G major, Op. 77, no. 1, by Haydn.

They play admirably. Their program of classic string quartets for Tuesday night is already sold out.

However, performance honors for the evening have to go to the university's Choral Union under the direction of Dr. James Chapman.

Music In Review

This year the festival is trying to make it on its own, and support such as the Union provides can hardly be measured.

It's a pity that festival economy has dictated no program. The members should have been listed in recognition of their artistry and their hours of rehearsal.

The Chamber Soloists provided great support for Dr. Chapman's conducting of the "Gloria" by Vivaldi, but the local singers truly distinguished themselves.

The bright opening "Gloria"; the crystal-clear polyphony with entrances as sharp as if they were shot from a gun; the solo work of Joanne Raymond, soprano, and Jill Levis,

---

Emerson Quartet: Future Plans

Along with fulfilling our remaining out-of-town concert commitments for the 1979-80 season and our Alice Tully Hall concert on May 7, we will travel to Madrid in April, all expenses paid, for one very important concert and a week of workshop classes. The trip is sponsored by the University of Corporate Presidents and the concert will be attended by the Spanish royalty and European impresarios (. Placido Domingo will appear on the same program). We hope this will afford us contacts that will help solidify our plans for a European tour sometime during the 1981-82 season.

This summer, the Vermont Mozart Festival offers us our first opportunity to perform the complete Beethoven cycle. We have been and will be studying and rehearsing for this throughout the season and for a solid two months right before the festival (July 13-August 2). Also this summer we will participate again in the Lincoln Center Institute for one week (July 7-13), with concerts and workshops.

The 1980-81 season will almost definitely include 40-50 touring concerts, 16 of which will be at the Smithsonian Institution in Washington, D.C.. Along with these concerts, we may perform the complete Beethoven cycle at Dumbarton Oaks in Washington, at five different colleges in the Denver area (a different program at each school), and hopefully elsewhere. In addition we will definitely give two concerts in Alice Tully Hall (March 15 and 22, 1981), performing the complete quartets of Bartok in commemoration of the centennial of his birth. Other plans: possible recording project at the Smithsonian, trying to interest major recording companies in us, a European tour sometime during the 1981-82 season; research and performance (and perhaps commission) of more American music, both old and new; Beethoven cycle in NY, 1981-82 season.

We realize that our plans may sound a bit presumptuous, but to really establish ourselves as important voices in the chamber music world we must be bold and think big. We can only promise, to ourselves especially, to work hard enough and perform well enough to fulfill our own and others' expectations.

Chapter 3

New arrival, new departures 1979-1983

PS: As we speak today about how we came together, you can see the four individual lines converging miraculously, a lot by chance, to form the ESQ. And when you look back over 25 years you see all of these threads coming together and forming something cohesive in terms of repertoire, in terms of how our career has expanded from the very beginning. It has an organic life of its own; we've been extremely lucky, but there has also been a design to it.

Getting to know David

Going back now, to trace David's emergence with us: I first knew about David from Oscar Shumsky. In my second year at Juilliard, Shumsky asked me if I would like to play the solo part in Haydn's Sinfonia Concertante with his orchestra in Madison, New Jersey, which was (and still is) called the Colonial Symphony. And I said "Sure!", willing to jump at anything. I didn't know the piece at all. There were four solo parts: violin, cello, oboe and bassoon. He mentioned who the wind players would be, both of whom I knew, and then he said "And the cello...I'm thinking about having a *local* boy do it. A very talented local boy - a high school student named David Finckel." I remember the first time I met David - we had a rehearsal in Shumsky's studio with the soloists. David has mentioned that he was very shy, and indeed he was. I don't remember him saying much of anything, but I do remember being struck by his playing. Our paths crossed a number of times between then and when David actually joined the Quartet. As Gene pointed out, David also played in the Empire Sinfonietta, so I knew David a bit from those two experiences.

After Gene and I went to the Queen Elisabeth Competition, I decided I wanted a summer without a lot of pressure. I had been to Marlboro the previous two summers and didn't want to have anything like that again for a while. I wanted to go someplace where I could just relax and play some chamber music. So I thought about the Craftsbury Chamber Players, where I had gone before and had met Guillermo. I called the director, Mary Anthony Cox, who said she'd love to have me back. I asked what players were coming that summer and she said, "There's a cellist named David Finckel." And I said, "Oh, I know David." So that summer was when I really got to know David well. We played chamber music together, hung out together, and decided to form a piano trio. It was mostly for fun, and we played a few concerts a year.

When Eric decided to leave the quartet, I knew that David would be the right person to replace him. The others had heard our trio and knew David a bit. So it wasn't like when Larry came in, when we really had no idea whom to choose and were auditioning a lot of people. In this case it was pretty clear that David was the right person, or at least a very good candidate.

LD: While I was at Juilliard I became friends with some Shumsky students and through them discovered how amazing their teacher was. I heard him play some recitals, and decided I'd do anything if I could to play in an orchestra under him. I had also become friends with his son, Eric, since Eric was also a viola player who studied with Lillian Fuchs. I played one concert in the Colonial Symphony, and David happened to be the soloist in the Rococo Variations. So that's the first time I actually heard him play. A lot came to the quartet through Shumsky - we were all influenced a great deal by him musically, and it was really because of him that we met David.

David auditions

DF: Because I became friends with the guys through the Empire Sinfonietta and the Colonial Symphony, I made the effort to go hear their quartet. My first chance was in the spring of 1979, near where I lived in New Jersey. The concert was in a low-ceilinged YMCA room (where I coincidentally had also heard the New York Chamber Soloists years earlier). Up to that point my musical experiences had been pretty user-friendly. The Emerson played Webern's Op. 5, the Fünf Stücke, preceded by a lengthy, intellectual explanation of the work which was delivered with great seriousness by one of the members. I remember feeling intimidated and thinking, "This quartet stuff is' too intense for me." And then they moved on to Bartok 5 and it only got worse. It was very stressful for me, and it would have been even more frightening had I known that I would soon be asked to get involved. I also went to their first Alice Tully Hall concert and felt the same way - kind of scared of them and of the music they tackled. But Phil and I continued to play trios together and we had a lot of fun.

1979-80 Fourth Season

September	**David Finckel** becomes the ESQ cellist
October	Beginning of the first series at **Renwick Gallery**, Smithsonian Institution, Washington, DC **Baltimore**, Maryland
November	Tour: **Buffalo**, NY; **Columbus**, Ohio; Dayton, Ohio; **Omaha**, Nebraska; **Kalamazoo**, Michigan; **Tulsa**, Oklahoma; **Salt Lake City**, Utah; **Vancouver**, British Columbia (first appearance in Canada); Edmonton, Alberta
January	Tour: **Provo**, Utah; **La Jolla**, California; **University of California, Riverside**, California; **UC Davis**, California; **UC Irvine**, California; **UC Los Angeles**, California; **Pittsburgh**, Pennsylvania
February	Tour: **Syracuse**, NY; **Gettysburgh**, Pennsylvania; **Annapolis**, Maryland; **Athens**, Georgia
May	Second Alice Tully Hall appearance, premiere of Mario **Davidovsky's Quartet No. 4**
July	First **Beethoven Cycle** at the Vermont Mozart Festival
August	**Martha's Vineyard**, Massachussetts **Maverick Concerts**, Woodstock, NY

1980-81 Fifth Season

September	Quartet begins association with the **Hartt School** in Hartford, Connecticut
November	Tour: **Lafayette**, Louisiana; **Montgomery**, Alabama; **Tulsa**, Oklahoma; **Enterprise**, Alabama; **Denver**, Colorado; **Phoenix**, Arizona
December	Washington, DC; Metropolitan Museum, NY
January	Princeton, New Jersey; Washington, DC; Hartt School, Hartford, Connecticut
February	Beethoven performances in Buffalo, NY, for the Slee Cycle; **Cornell University**; Ithaca, NY
March	First-ever performance of six Bartok Quartets in a single evening "Bartok Marathon" at Alice Tully Hall, Lincoln Center **Union College**, Schenectady, NY
April	Quartet begins annual appearances at **Stanford University**, California, with the Bartok Cycle
July	First appearances at **Spoleto Festivals** in Charleston, SC, and Italy
August	First appearance at the **Tanglewood Music Festival** First appearance at the **Ottawa Festival**
August 30	**Marriage of Eugene Drucker and Roberta Cooper.**

Later, in April, Phil called me up and said he wanted to come over and talk with me. He showed up at my apartment with a bottle of Scotch and dragged me into the next-to-smallest room in my house. We started drinking and he told me that Eric was going to leave and suggested that I try out for the quartet. He laid a pile of audition pieces on me, one of which was the dreaded Webern Fünf Stücke. At that point I had never thought of playing in a quartet and I had studied and performed approximately one string quartet my whole life. But by that time in the conversation I'd had enough to drink and said I'd give it a try. There were only a few days until the audition.

The audition was a turning point for me. I was thrilled playing with a group that had already had so much experience, and whose individual members played on such a high level. It sounded great to me, right away, without ever having rehearsed. I played Mozart quartets with difficult solos, the Ravel Quartet, and the Webern. It was a very challenging audition but I felt that I had connected musically with the group. I wasn't totally sure what they were thinking, but in a matter of days they asked me to join the quartet, and I said yes.

From the moment of the audition I knew that I wanted to be in the quartet, if they would have me. I was one of many struggling New York freelancers waiting by the phone for gigs that I didn't particularly enjoy playing. When this opportunity came along - a group of fantastic players offering me a season of 50 or 60 concerts - I'd have been crazy to say no. I went to Marlboro that summer while they finished up with Eric, and then we started working together in the fall. My first concert with the Emerson Quartet was at the Muhlenburg College Center for the Arts, in Muhlenburg, Pennsylvania, in October 1979.

ED: 1979-80 was David's first season with the quartet and he learned around 70 works, which gives you a very good idea of how ambitious we were so early in our career. A highlight of that season came in May 1980, when we played our second concert at Alice Tully Hall. The program included the world premiere of

Mario Davidovsky's 4th Quartet, plus the Ravel and Beethoven's Op. 127.

The first Beethoven cycle

We played the Beethoven quartet again a couple of months later in our first-ever Beethoven cycle at the Vermont Mozart Festival. We were still a very young quartet to be attempting the whole cycle. Mel Kaplan had cajoled us into doing it, and we had certain doubts, but in retrospect it was one of the most important opportunities ever offered to us.

DF: We played the Beethoven concerts in all kinds of locations - outdoors, indoors, etc. as one is likely to do at summer festivals. It was harrowing - there were bugs, wind and trains. I distinctly remember missing one of the tough page turns in our first performance of Op. 131. I actually worried that I might be fired. But the support and encouragement coming from the festival community enabled us to get through the cycle in one piece.

The Bartok Marathon

ED: Our next repertoire milestone was Phil's brainchild. The Bartok centenary year (1981) was approaching and there were many Bartok concerts being presented that season in New York and elsewhere. We tried to figure out what we could do that would be special and stand out from the crowd. After listening to the Juilliard Quartet's recordings in a single sitting, Phil came up with the idea to play all six Bartok Quartets in chronological order in one concert. We thought he'd gone crazy.

Normally, when the Bartok quartets are played in two concerts, you have to break up the compositional order. But playing them in one concert gave us the opportunity to trace Bartok's compositional development chronologically, over 31 years of his creative life. It would be like hearing a musical biography of a composer in one evening, and within the six quartets there's a tremendous

variety of sonority and structure. We decided to take the risk, and wagered that most of the audience would stick with us and hopefully have an unforgettable experience (in the good sense!).

Bartok's quartets also reflect the history of the first half of the 20th century. Two of the quartets, the 2nd and the 6th, are related to the two World Wars. The 2nd quartet, composed from 1915-1917, reflects the violence and dislocation of WW I, and the 6th quartet was written on the eve of WW II, when Bartok already knew that he would be forced to leave his homeland.

DF: The Bartok Marathon concert (as it came to be called) in March 1981 at Alice Tully Hall was probably the scariest concert of my career to that date, since no one had ever attempted this program. We really didn't know if it was possible or even sensible. Fortunately we made it through. The intense concentration of our listeners helped enormously, and they gave us a long ovation at the end. I believe that this concert marked the birth of an audience in New York that we could call our own - one that has remained with us and will come hear us try new ideas, and perhaps even forgive us a failure or two.

The Bartok Marathon concert seemed to put the Emerson on the map of the quartet world. We stuck our necks way, way out, and everyone took notice. It taught us that if we wanted to have a life in a quartet, or even in classical music, we had to be prepared to take risks.

Spoleto

In May of 1981 the quartet was invited for the first time to the Spoleto Festivals in Charleston, South Carolina, and Spoleto, Italy. It was our first contact with an international musical public, and it was a great thrill for us to be in Italy for two whole weeks. All the musicians lived with Italian families, and we tasted, for the first time, the delirious enjoyment that so many Americans experience upon discovering the Italian way of life.

Through Spoleto we became acquainted with a stellar selection of musicians, such as Jean-Yves Thibaudet, Joshua Bell, Yefim Bronfman, Carter Brey, and more. In addition, the organizers - Charles Wadsworth (who was at the time also Artistic Director of The Chamber Music Society of Lincoln Center) and violist Scott Nickrenz proved to be important figures in the early stages of our career.

We returned once to Italy and several times to Charleston, and reluctantly had to give up going as time became shorter and schedules became tighter. But I have rarely enjoyed myself as much anywhere - musically, socially, or gastronomically.

The Chamber Music Society of Lincoln Center

LD: As David mentioned, Charles Wadsworth was the Artistic Director of the Society, which was then acknowledged as the premier chamber music organization in New York, and possibly in the United States as well. He had heard us prior to the festival on a radio broadcast in a performance of the Debussy Quartet, and, being a real French-music enthusiast, not only paid close attention but apparently liked what he heard. After hearing us live in Charleston, he invited us to join The Chamber Music Society of Lincoln Center. It was a thrilling milestone in our career: at last, an association with one of America's most respected musical organizations, in one of New York's most important venues. It would give us the opportunity to play for thousands of listeners, with some of the most distinguished colleagues in the business. And what do you think we played for our debut with the Society, in December 1982? The Debussy Quartet!

Our happy and fruitful association with the Society continued for a number of seasons, after which we needed to part ways in order to fulfill more engagements out of town. But we have remained close friends and admirers of the Society and have returned several times to perform as guest artists. Our musical associations with the Society's current members, among them violist Paul Neubauer, cellists Fred Sherry and Gary Hoffman, and of course Artistic Director-clarinetist David Shifrin, are quite special for us.

Hartt

ED: Another important association was our residency at the Hartt School of Music, part of the University of Hartford in Connecticut, dating back to 1980. In Phil's introduction about his own musical studies he mentioned Rafael Druian, the concertmaster of the Cleveland Orchestra. By 1980, Druian was teaching at the Hartt School and it was through him that we were able to audition there and be engaged the following season as Quartet-in-Residence, a position which we have maintained for over two decades. We gradually expanded our involvement and have been full-time faculty since 1986. It's been satisfying to see a number of extremely talented groups who worked under our tutelage go on to make formidable careers of their own - for example the first group, the St. Lawrence String Quartet, who worked with us in the early 90s. They were followed by the Avalon, the Canberra and the Coolidge Quartets, the Adaskin String Trio, and now the Diabelli Quartet. We also inaugurated an annual competition at the school for students to join us for ensemble works - quintets, sextets, even string quartets with one of us sitting out.

Other concerts

LD: In April 1981 we played the Bartok cycle in two concerts at Stanford University and we also conducted various outreach events for their "Lively Arts" program. Just this past April in 2001 we were feted very generously by the Lively Arts Committee and we played in Stanford on the exact 20th anniversary of our first concert there. We've made many life-long friends in that community.

In the fall of 1981 we began a four-year series of mini-residencies at Middlebury College in Vermont in association with the great musicologist H. C. Robbins Landon, who gave lectures before each concert. The first year, October 1981, we played programs featuring quartets of Haydn and Mozart. The next season we played the Beethoven cycle, and the third year we played a wide variety of romantic music ranging from Schubert to Brahms and Dvorak.

In the fall of 1984 we completed the series with 20th-century music.

ED: We repeated the Bartok Marathon at New York's Symphony Space in early 1983, as part of an eight-concert series created by Phil called "Music for Survival". The concerts helped an organization known as Performing Artists for Nuclear Disarmament, and our subsequent benefit performances have supported a variety of causes: the fight against children's diseases, the eradication of world hunger, care for the aged and infirm, and education.

Summer festivals

Our first summer festival besides the Vermont Mozart Festival was the Caramoor Festival in Caramoor, New York, where we played in the summer of 1978, before David was in the group. In 1981 we played our first concert at Tanglewood and returned in 1983 - that was the first concert I played on the instrument that I still use, my Stradivarius.

DF: We also participated in the Casals Festival in Puerto Rico in 1982 and 1983. I found my first great cello there, my Guadagnini - it belonged to a member of the Puerto Rico Symphony. At that point we had begun the difficult task of acquiring really first-rate instruments, and we were helped by a number of extraordinarily generous individuals who

△ The second Naumburg concert, Alice Tully Hall, Lincoln Center, May 1980

1981-82 Sixth Season

October	First of four yearly series at **Middlebury College**, Vermont, in tandem with lectures by H.C. Robbins Landon
	Dallas Chamber Music Society
November	Beethoven cycle, Hartt School, Hartford, Connecticut; Duluth, Minnesota; Ames, Iowa
December	Metropolitan Museum, NY; Washington DC
January	Eugene, Oregon; UC Berkeley, California; Washington DC
February	Beethoven Cycle in the Denver area: Denver, **Boulder, Arvada, Fort Collins and Laramie, Wyoming**
March	Baltimore, Maryland, **Boca Raton, Florida**
April	**High Point,** North Carolina; **Moorehead and Louisville, Kentucky**
June	First appearance at **Casals Festival, Puerto Rico**
	David Finckel acquires a **J.B. Guadagnini cello** (1754, Milan)
July	**"Making Music",** a documentary about the quartet, filmed on Martha's Vineyard

1982-83 Seventh Season

October	Second series at Middlebury College, Vermont
November	Philip Setzer acquires a **Santa Serafino violin** (Milan)
December	First concert as members of **The Chamber Music Society of Lincoln Center,** NY.
	Pittsburgh Chamber Music Society
January	**WETA television program "In Residence",** filmed at the Renwick Gallery of the Smithsonian Institution, Washington, DC
March	Bartok Marathon at Symphony Space in NY, "Music for Survival"
April	**First European tour,** lasting 34 days, through 10 countries. The tour included a "Bartok Marathon" for the quartet's debut in **Frankfurt.** First concert in **Paris, Salle Gaveau.** Also Munich, Stockholm, **Budapest, Amsterdam, Recklinghausen, Istanbul**
June	Eugene Drucker acquires an **Antonio Stradivarius violin** (1686, Cremona)
	Tanglewood Music Festival, with Boston Symphony Chamber Players
July	First appearances at the **Aspen Music Festival.** Premiere of **Maurice Wright's String Quartet**
August	First appearance, **Mostly Mozart Festival,** NY, with Richard Stoltzman

made gifts and organized consortiums of contributors. (We did go into debt, too...!)

Aspen

LD: In 1983 we made our first appearances at the Aspen Music Festival and School. We've played there almost every season since and consider it our summer home-away-from-home. Aspen has been generous to the quartet in every way, and has hosted all of our big projects, from Beethoven to Bartok to Shostakovich and contemporary repertoire. Our involvement with the Aspen Music School includes annual quartet master classes, coaching of the groups in the school's Quartet Program, and private teaching. The festival has also provided us numerous opportunities for solo recitals and appearances with orchestra.

ESQ in the movies

ED: In the summer of 1982, when we were playing some concerts with our colleagues from the Smithsonian on Martha's Vineyard, a film was made about the quartet. It was called "Making Music". Robert and Marjorie Potts, Vineyard residents, were the producers, and the camera man worked for the famous television journalist Bill Moyers. They did a wonderful job and made a visually striking film which won various awards. Another early visual documentation of our work was made by Washington's WETA in January 1983 at one of the concerts we played at the Renwick Gallery.

DF: In the summer of 1983, at Aspen, I was invited to a party with some students. One of them was named David Stern. He took a phone call during the evening and came back to say that his Dad had just enjoyed the Emerson's Beethoven Op. 59 #3 on TV. It was the film Gene just mentioned, and his Dad was Isaac Stern, which I hadn't known at the time. It was the first time Stern heard us.

Close relationships

DF: Between 1979 and 1983 we began playing in many of the places at which we continue to appear, and where we have established important personal relationships. For example, in Denver, during our Beethoven cycle in the area, we were housed with local families with whom we have since become life-long friends. Our friends from communities such as Denver follow us to concerts in various places - sometimes as far away as Germany. It's been an extraordinarily fortunate part of our career that we have established an international coalition of families that support us musically, socially, and emotionally.

ED: Another place this has happened is in the Champlain Valley area of Vermont. When we started playing there in the summer of 1977 we became very friendly with people in the community, especially a few families with whom we often stayed when we came back to play concerts in the area. When we were at the Mozart Festival we also had the extraordinary experience of staying at Shelburne Farms, which is now a very luxurious inn, but at that time the mansion on the grounds of the farm was available to us to stay in. It was a breathtakingly beautiful spot overlooking Lake Champlain. Whenever I go there it still strikes me as one of the most beautiful places I've ever seen.

DF: I know we're getting into trouble here, because we'll inevitably leave some people and places out. We should mention the Stanford University crowd, connected to the Lively Arts Series. We've been presented so many times by the organization - all our major projects - and enjoyed such warm relationships with that community.

PS: When we look back at our career, we remember the many wonderful organizations who have done great things for us along the way. There will always be a special feeling for the places that really took a chance on us in the beginning, not only hiring us once, but having us back a number of times before we had really made it, before they were sure they could sell tickets. They simply believed in what we were doing and they were able to promote us in that way.

DF: Soon after joining the quartet, I met extraordinary people who had become friends of the Emerson. Among them: in New York, Irvine and Elizabeth Flinn, and Edwin and Kathe Williamson; in New Jersey, Joseph and Susan Zuch; in California, Paul and Iris Brest, and William and Judy Sloan; and in Washington DC, Robert and Gerri Josephs. These generous individuals supported the quartet in a variety of ways, making it possible for us to move forward in our career from one level to the next. We'll always be grateful for their belief in us in our early stages, and for their continued friendship. ๑

△   Woodside, California, near Stanford University, April 1981.

Photograph by Stanley Golden

Chapter 4

Music capitals 1983-87

European management

LD: We had been playing for six years in the United States and Canada and were anxious to have the opportunity to tour abroad. The Juilliard Quartet had world-wide management, of course, and their management in Germany was Concerto Winderstein. The company head, Dr. Hans-Dieter Göhre, had been seeking to manage a young quartet, possibly from America. He asked Robert Mann to suggest a group and Mann mentioned us. Hans-Dieter had already been pressed on our account by Melvin Kaplan - another good choice on Mel's part. Bending to the persuasion of our two allies, Hans-Dieter decided to give us our first tour.

DF: We first met Hans-Dieter at the Mayflower Hotel in New York and expected a white-haired, formal German businessman. We all wore jackets and

Photograph by John Russell

ties. And suddenly we were sitting with a very handsome and cool-looking guy, late forties, chic leather jacket, no tie, laughing and having a great time. It was a fantastic introduction to what was to become a big career in Europe, and the beginning of a great relationship with Hans-Dieter that continues to this day.

The first European tour

ED: The first European tour was in the spring of 1983. It lasted nearly five weeks and we played in ten different countries. We visited four of the countries under the auspices of the United States Information Service, but our concerts in the other six were arranged through Concerto Winderstein.

LD: I'll never forget that tour, particularly the first concert. It was in the Concertgebouw in Amsterdam, one of the most distinguished halls in the world, and up to this point we had been playing mostly for American audiences. It was absolutely frightening, thinking about the tradition...and I'll never forget the quiet and the attentiveness of that audience. I could hear my heart beating. I was never so scared in my life! People were sitting on the stage - we weren't used to that either - this intense crowd all around us, some of them actually looking at our music while we played! Later, in Germany, the concert was recorded and they had many microphones surrounding us. Just getting into our seats was a great effort, and once again, the people were so quiet. We got a fantastic response. And playing so many encores - that was new to us! We'd take a bow , come back, take another bow, come back. After the fourth bow we knew we had to start playing encores. We weren't prepared for this. We played and they still wanted more. We didn't know what to do. It just didn't stop.

DF: I can remember scrambling around backstage, frantically looking through our music for more to play...

LD: So we got used to that and quickly learned that you had to play two, possibly three encores at all the concerts. And, they were very interested in all the details: which edition you used, what instrument you played, which strings you used....

PS: Speaking about traveling internationally, there are many different ways an audience acts, and also reacts to what you're doing (this is true also to some extent in the US). For instance, in Budapest, we played the whole Bartok 3rd Quartet as an encore. They went crazy and were applauding in a rhythmic pattern: strong, weak, strong, weak. In Amsterdam, if they really like your performance, they'll give you a standing ovation before the intermission. We were very surprised - we thought maybe they had to get to the bathroom quickly!

LD: I have a theory that has evolved over the years, which has to do with international styles of performing and the kinds of halls in different countries. When we first went to Europe it was a big question for us, how we should approach the performance. We quickly learned that many of Europe's great halls are very resonant - the Concertgebouw, or the Musikverein in Vienna, for example. They almost amplify the sound, meaning that we didn't need to play so "big" in them. We were used to the United States, where we often play in bigger and usually drier spaces. Also, in America you often have to "prove yourself", and earn the attention of the audience. In Europe it's more likely that the public has lived with the music and they know it well. So you can pull back and focus more on internal quality.

1983-84 Eighth Season

September   First appearance at **South Mountain Concerts, Pittsfield,**
Massachusetts; Kennedy Center, Washington DC; **Yale University,**
New Haven, Connecticut

October   Pittsburgh Chamber Music Society with violist Walter Trampler

November   Third series at Middlebury College, Vermont,
with H.C. Robbins Landon
Concerto program (Brahms Double, Mozart Sinfonia Concertante)
with the **Asheville, North Carolina Symphony;**
Concert for the Coalition for Nuclear Disarmament, with Lilian
Kallir, NY; **Indianapolis,** Indiana

December   **West Palm Beach,** Florida, with pianist Claude Frank
Durham, North Carolina; Cleveland, Ohio; Lincoln Center Chamber
Music Society, NY

January   **Brooklyn Academy of Music, Brooklyn,** NY; Washington DC; Hartt
School, Hartford, Connecticut, **Eureka Springs,** Arkansas; Met
Museum, NY

February   **New Orleans, Louisiana; St. Thomas, Virgin Islands; Winter Park,**
Florida; UCLA, California; Stanford University, California;
UC Berkeley, California

March   European tour: **Mannheim, Zurich, Vienna.** London debut at the
Wigmore Hall

April   Recording sessions: **Romantic quartets for Book-of-the-Month Club**
Records, NY

May   Premiere of **George Tsontakis' String Quartet** for The Chamber
Music Society of Lincoln Center, Alice Tully Hall

1984-85 Ninth Season

September   German Tour: Ludwigsburg Festival; Leverkusen; first appearance
at the Hotel Römerbad, Badenweiler;
Berlin, Munich, **Iserlohn, Neumarkt, Schwäbisch Hall**

October   **New Paltz,** NY; **Columbia,** Maryland; **Lawrence,** Kansas

November   Fourth series at Middlebury College, Vermont,
with H.C. Robbins Landon

January   **St. Louis, Missouri; Chicago, Illinois; St. Paul, Minnesota**

February   Premiere of the **Cecil Effinger quartet,** Denver, Colorado; **Pompano**
Beach, Florida; **Oklahoma City,** Oklahoma

New York and London

DF: During this period we were fortunate to play in the major venues of New York and London. Even more fortunate for us has been the continuing relationships we have enjoyed with all of them. Our large repertoire projects have been hosted by great concert halls in both cities, and the exposure that has afforded us is responsible, to a large degree, for where we are today.

PS: Our most visible New York concerts began with the Naumburg Award appearances at **Lincoln Center,** and we have appeared there regularly ever since. A Beethoven cycle, the Bartok Marathon, and various other series have been presented in Alice Tully Hall, and we have enjoyed almost annual concerts at the Mostly Mozart Festival in Avery Fisher Hall since our first appearance on that series in 1983. Jane Moss, Lincoln Center's Vice-President for Programming, has been not only a major creative force within the organization but has also become a real collaborator with the Emerson Quartet, helping us develop projects like "The Noise of Time". As we celebrate our 25th anniversary season there with encore performances of "The Noise of Time" and a special series of three concerts, we look forward to an exciting future with Lincoln Center and are grateful for the enormous artistic possibilities this relationship affords us.

LD: **Carnegie Hall,** the one and only, has been equally receptive to our projects, and we consider ourselves privileged to have performed in the great space so often. Under the late Judith Arron, the quartet gave its Carnegie debut with the Bartok Marathon, and we have returned many times with important repertoire and favorite guest artists. We also have plans involving Carnegie's new performance space, Zankel Hall. Our good friends whom we first met at Aspen, Robert Harth and Ara Guzelimian, now steer the venerable ship with expert hands.

ED: Our first appearance at the **Metropolitan Museum** in December 1981 was the only concert we played in New York during that season. But a couple of years later we had a series there for two seasons running: the first one featured late Beethoven and late Schubert, and the other mixed programs. We gradually made our way around the major New York venues.

DF: Our first concert in London, in March 1984, introduced us to the legendary **Wigmore Hall**, and to its director William Lyne. We have since played on the hall's various series, performed for live broadcasts by BBC 3, and presented half of our Shostakovich cycle there in the spring of 2000. The hall is an acoustical wonder, a temple of chamber music to its devoted audience.

LD: London's **South Bank Centre** has hosted not only our Beethoven and Bartok cycles, but is hosting our 25th anniversary series as well. Invited first by Graham Sheffield, and subsequently by Amelia Freedman, the quartet looks upon the Centre as a favorite venue which has helped us achieve a strong identity in the United Kingdom.

PS: **The Barbican Centre**, a more recent venue for us, hosted two concerts of middle and late Shostakovich quartets as part of the cycle we performed in 2000. We were impressed by the large audience who listened so intently, and we were grateful to our host, Graham Sheffield, not only for presenting the concerts but also for arranging pre-concert talks with our Shostakovich annotator Paul Epstein and the musicologist Gerard McBurney. The lighting and visuals employed also lent impact, and we are grateful for the Centre's belief in and backing of our project. The Barbican Theatre also hosted, in the summer of 2001, our theatrical collaboration with Complicité, The Noise of Time.

International connections

ED: On an early European tour in 1984, we met an extraordinary man named Klaus Lauer who had come to hear our concert in Zurich. His family has

owned and operated a luxury hotel, the **Hotel Römerbad** in Badenweiler, Germany, for over a century. Klaus inaugurated an important music festival at the Römerbad, which happens several times a year: the Musiktage, as they are called. We made our first appearances there as part of the Musiktage in March 1986, though we played there informally as early as September, 1984.

DF: What connected us initially to Klaus were our common musical friends: the late soprano Jan DeGaetani, the pianist Gilbert Kalish, and the Juilliard

March	Lawrence Dutton acquires a **Pietro Giovanni Mantegazza viola** (1796, Milan)
	European tour: **Messina, Milan, Verona, Amsterdam, Utrecht, The Hague, Paris, Lübeck, Nürnburg**
June 15	**Marriage of Philip Setzer and Linda Dannhauser (neé Levine)**
July	Premiere of **Ronald Caltabiano's String Quartet** at the Aspen Music Festival, Colorado
	First appearance at the **Ravinia Festival**

1985-86 Tenth Season

September 15	**David Finckel marries pianist Wu Han**
October	First tour of **Japan**
November	**Raleigh**, North Carolina; **Auburh**, Alabama; **Oberlin**, Ohio
December	**Toronto**, Canada
January	Release of the quartet's recording of **eight romantic quartets** for Book-of-the-Month Club records: Brahms c minor, Schumann A major, Debussy, Ravel, Dvorak "American", Smetana, Tchaikovsky D major, Borodin
	San Francisco, California; **Houston**, Texas; **Anchorage**, Alaska
February	**Gainesville**, Florida; **Brattleboro**, Vermont
	European tour: **Bremen, Hamburg, Mannheim**, Munich, Frankfurt, **Florence, Innsbruck, Linz, Lausanne, St. Gallen**
April	**Baton Rouge**, Louisiana; **Montclair**, New Jersey
May	**Montreal**, Canada
June	European tour: **Bologna, Feldkirch (Schubertiade), Passau, Iserlohn, Schwetzingen**, with cellist Antonio Meneses

Quartet. The reason these artists were such favorites of Klaus's is that they would perform new music for him. Klaus's curiosity for the "new" in all the arts is inextinguishable, and his passion for personal expansion and artistic exploration has endeared him to the world's greatest living composers. Carter, Boulez, Kurtag, Nono, Rihm - and many others have all stayed at his hotel and had Musiktage festivals dedicated to their works. It was Klaus who introduced us to the music of Wolfgang Rihm, and commissioned his Ninth Quartet for us. So Klaus Lauer is directly responsible for challenging the quartet and expanding our imaginations and abilities, and enriching our lives through his extraordinary artistic vision, friendship and hospitality.

PS: When we first went to **Japan** in 1985 we had no recordings out that were available there, so we were really not well known. The halls were not full and the audiences didn't seem very connected to what we were doing. But we would find, talking to people afterwards, that they were extremely interested in what we were doing, and just didn't show it in an obvious way. Now, since we've had recordings out in Japan, we have a lot more success with big audiences and I think chamber music has caught on there. In principle, however, you can never truly judge from the reaction of an audience whether they are really enthusiastic or not, because people in different parts of the world show their feelings in different ways.

DF: **Australia**, where we played for the first time in 1987, is a very special place in the world. The familiar Australian warmth and friendliness characterize their music-loving public as well. Acoustically excellent concert halls such as the Sydney Opera House and the Queen Elizabeth Hall in Melbourne, discriminating audiences such as the one that listened to our Bartok Marathon on a hot night in the Sydney Town Hall, and the hospitality of the national presenting organization, Musica Viva, all combine to make Australia one of our favorite places to tour. o

An impromptu performance of gratitude for the kitchen staff of the Hotel Römerbad

Chapter 5

Prelude to a recording career

Confronting the classics

ED: In the spring of 1984 we very quickly recorded eight string quartets for the Book-of-the-Month Club. That recording didn't come out until 1986, when it was well received. The Book-of-the-Month Club series was eventually re-issued by Deutsche Grammophon, when we were under contract with DG, as four separate CD's, and they're still very popular.

DF: These were our first recordings of standard repertoire. The opportunity proved daunting in many respects. Fortunately, the company had the good sense to hire Max Wilcox to produce for us. He had been our first choice anyway, since we had grown up admiring his recordings of the Guarneri Quartet, among others. He was vastly experienced - already a legend in the business.

Photograph by Stephanie Berger; courtesy of The Chamber Music Society of Lincoln Center

We recorded at what now seems like a breakneck pace: two movements before lunch and two after lunch, and that was it, one day per quartet. And they were technically difficult pieces! Somehow Max got us through it, and when we came out of it all, we not only had made what turned out to be good records, but also had a great new friend in Max, who later shepherded us through the Beethoven Quartets and other projects.

Max Wilcox challenged the Emerson in a unique and unexpected way. He came to the recording sessions (and also to our prior rehearsals!) with very strong opinions of how the music should be played, and never hesitated to let us know if he thought we were making musical mistakes. This being our first recording, and knowing his experience working with the Guarneri, we were mightily intimidated by his presence at first, until we realized that through his questioning, examining and sometimes challenging our interpretive decisions he was actually helping us build up our strengths and convictions. And the tape would always tell the truth, so we had an impartial judge. Max's strongest points were his excellent musical taste, his ability to recognize a great take, and his ability to make us play our best. We were lucky to have such a privileged experience in our first recordings of standard literature.

Beethoven cycles

PS: In 1986-87 we celebrated our tenth season by performing the Beethoven cycle at least three times - in and around the Los Angeles area (the organizers named it "Beethoven Odyssey" in the hope that it would sound like fun to drive around to different corners of the city to hear it!). We also presented the cycle at Stanford University in Palo Alto, and at Lincoln Center's Alice Tully Hall, presented by The Chamber Music Society of Lincoln Center. It was our first Beethoven cycle in New York.

Radio exposure

ED: Another important association at that time was Minnesota Public Radio's "Saint Paul Sunday" program, which really helped us become familiar to the American radio public. We first recorded for SPS in the summer of '87 and have done probably ten shows for them since that time.

DF: One thing we can thankful to Saint Paul Sunday for is that they have always devoted themselves to the projects that we're involved in. For example, they were interested in our musical relationship to Oscar Shumsky, and came all the way to New York to record him and us together. For our Beethoven cycle, they not only produced exclusive Beethoven shows but created an entire Web site having to do with Beethoven and the quartets. They followed us through our Shostakovich project. They've been real creative partners in helping us get this music to the widest possible audience. For that we are very grateful to them. They are as dedicated a bunch of music lovers as you will find anywhere in the world. The Saint Paul Sunday team, virtually the same cast of wonderful characters since we have been going there, is headed by our dear friends: producer Mary Lee and host Bill McGlaughlin.

ED: We also had a lot of exposure on National Public Radio through our involvement with the Spoleto Festival and The Chamber Music Society of Lincoln Center. All of the concerts in Charleston and many in New York were taped for broadcast, as were our concerts at the Smithsonian for many years. Through NPR we met brilliant producers and hosts, such as Steve Zakar and Martin Goldsmith, who took our work, and music in general, very seriously. So even though we did not embark on a major recording career until 1987, we became widely known to people who could not come to hear us live, thanks to Public Radio. ◦

Chapter 6

Deutsche Grammophon 1987

Waiting for the right company

PS: One of the difficulties in the early part of our career was finding the right recording situation. We were playing over 100 concerts a year for several seasons around the world before we had an exclusive recording contract with a major company. Part of the reason is that we had offers that we decided to turn down. And I think we made the right decision not to jump at things too quickly, not to record a lot of the standard repertoire too early. The right scenario finally did arrive in 1987 through our management's discussions with various recording companies - DG made an offer which we happily accepted. And we began a long association with the "Yellow Label".

I remember Larry calling up very excitedly and playing a recording over the phone of a message from Hans-Dieter, who had worked very hard to get us the contract. He left a screaming message on Larry's answering machine informing us that DG had decided to go with the ESQ. It was a very, very happy moment in our career.

I remember the excitement of going to Hamburg to sign our first recording contract - of meeting all of the department heads and getting a lot of congratulations, but also getting some advice from the president who said to us, as we were walking down the street, "You know, you have to do what you can do now. Do it quickly because there's always another group coming along who's going to take your place." We had been riding high, and this brought us quickly back down to earth. But it was tremendously exciting nevertheless, the idea that we were now entering a stage in our career where we could record. The timing couldn't have been better historically, because CD's were just coming out, digital recording was just beginning, and major labels needed repertoire recorded with the new technology. There was a real boom going on in the industry and we were handed a major opportunity.

The first Deutsche Grammophon recording

DF: The quartet was very concerned with how and where we would make our debut recording. We organized a quick tour of possible recording locations in the New York area - actually a large radius, which included Troy, New York, a good three hours north of New York City. Troy has a wonderful old hall above the Troy Savings Bank. And the coincidence was that the engineer we employed to do

sound tests for us was Da-Hong Seetoo, who is now our recording engineer and producer for DG. We selected the Troy Music Hall as the site of our first recording.

DG was very cooperative - shipped all the engineers and equipment up there, on our recommendation - and we spent a week recording Schubert's "Death and the Maiden" and Beethoven's Op. 95. It was incredibly hot, and there was an unfamiliar crew of German technicians and producers. But we felt that the recording was very successful and we had a beautiful cover

Photograph by Andreas Laible/DGG

1986-87 Eleventh Season

October	Premiere of Gunther Schuller's Quartet No. 3, for the Syracuse Friends of Chamber Music
January - March	First New York Beethoven cycle at Alice Tully Hall, Lincoln Center
January	Beethoven cycle, Los Angeles area, California.
February	Beethoven cycle, Stanford University, Palo Alto, California
March	Quartet signs exclusive recording contract with Deutsche Grammophon
July	First taping for Minnesota Public Radio's St. Paul Sunday
August	First appearances at the Salzburg Festival, Lucerne Festival, Helsinki, Ascona

1987-88 Twelfth Season

September	First tour of Australia, and second tour of Japan First concerts in Hawaii
October 16	Marriage of Lawrence Dutton and Elizabeth Lim
January	First Deutsche Grammophon release: Schubert "Death and the Maiden", D810; Beethoven Op. 95 Premiere of John Harbison's Quartet No. 2, Harvard Musical Association
January 24	Linda and Philip Setzer's daughter, Katia Elena, is born
February	Tour with Oscar Shumsky and Menahem Pressler, playing an all-French program including Chausson's Concerto for violin, piano, and string quartet
April-May	European tour: Viersen, Dusseldorf, Recklinghausen, Duisburg, Hamburg, Lübeck, Amsterdam, Nantes, Paris, Pistoia, Vienna

picture taken by Christian Steiner. We put everything we had into that first recording - fortunately it met with a lot of favorable criticism and the company seemed happy to continue with us.

Bartok

Our second recording project was the Bartok Quartets. For this one we selected the American Academy of Arts and Letters, which we had known from our Book-of-the-Month Club recordings. DG sent over a very distinguished producer, Wolf Erichson, who did a marvelous job, along with a wonderful technician named Peter Laenger. They made a great team and made us a great record.

ED: In the midst of the Bartok recording, when we were supposed to record the 3rd Quartet, we had to postpone that session because Phil's daughter Katia was born. We all decided to dedicate that recording to her. She was the quartet's first baby!

LD: The recording went on to win the Gramophone Magazine Record of the Year award and later two Grammys, including Best Classical Album. The Emerson was the first, and I believe still the only chamber ensemble ever to win the Best Classical award.

An amazing trip to accept the Gramophone award

LD: In order for us to get to the Gramophone awards ceremony in London at the Savoy Hotel it was necessary to take the Concorde over and back. The awards ceremony was at noon and we had a concert the same night in upstate New York. We were then met at Kennedy Airport by a private jet to take us directly up to Potsdam. We managed to fly to London, the next day have the awards

△ The quartet and Stephen Paul accept the Gramophone Award for Best
Classical Album, Savoy Hotel, London, 1989

ceremony, fly back on the Concorde, be shuttled up to Potsdam NY, play our concert, and be taken back home that evening. Pretty amazing stuff!

PS: And throughout all of it, my daughter was in the hospital. She had been diagnosed with Juvenile Diabetes...

ED: I remember that was a very difficult time for you and Linda.

DF: DG also graciously embraced our previously-recorded set of romantic quartets for Book-Of-The-Month Club. We were very grateful to the company for taking over these recordings and making them available world-wide. And eventually DG welcomed Max Wilcox, our producer for those early recordings, to record important releases for us - the Beethoven cycle and the Pressler recordings among them.

LD: The relationship that we've had with DG has been so special because they have allowed us to record all the great repertoire for string quartets - I mean, we haven't recorded it all, but they've never had an issue with what we wanted to do. We are now approaching the beginning of our fourth contract period with the company.

DF: We are enormously grateful to DG, a company which has not only remained loyal to the four of us (through many changes of their own administrative staff) but which has also stayed a true and principled course during these times of great instability in the classical record market. We've never been made to dumb down our product or our image to increase sales - the company has found a way to remain successful while at the same time marketing great music for what it is. They have shown great courage and faith, and we consider ourselves the most fortunate quartet in the world to still be with them. o

Chapter 7

Meeting mentors 1987-90

Introduction

DF: One of the most pivotal experiences in a performer's life is suddenly finding yourself onstage with your teachers or mentors, no longer as students but as colleagues. The years just after our tenth anniversary brought us full circle with some of our most important influences, and pushed us all to new levels of artistic self-expectation.

The Guarneri Quartet

As high school students we all had heard the Guarneri's first recordings. I learned the Beethoven Quartets from listening to them. Their solid musicianship, born of their own years of being mentored by musicians like Casals, Szell, etc. combined with their beauty of sound, phenomenal technical accuracy and their personal attractiveness, really elevated the public's quartet awareness to new heights.

LD: It was a thrill to be invited to play the Mendelssohn Octet with them on one of their annual series of concerts at Alice Tully Hall, in 1987. There's nothing quite like sitting next to people you've idolized for many years and suddenly making music together. It was a terrific night for us.

Isaac Stern and Bartok at Carnegie Hall

DF: Our Carnegie Hall debut in 1988 consisted of the Bartok Marathon concert, concurrent with the release of our Bartok recordings. The occasion was also our first meeting with the late Isaac Stern, on stage at our rehearsal. He came in during our run-through of the Third Quartet, ambled up onto the stage and stood between our two violinists, peering at the music while they were frantically scraping through the final pages.

PS: We were playing a passage which is written in minor 9ths, which is a half step wider than an octave. The interval sounds like a really out-of-tune octave, and I turned around and jokingly said, " How do you like my octaves?" Never at a loss for words, he replied, "I've played octaves like that." It sort of broke the tension!

DF: It was really quite a moment, finding ourselves on that stage being scrutinized by Stern. But he supported our efforts and was very helpful getting us into the best position on the stage. That was a very important day. Our close relationship with him continued, teaching together in many countries, performing with him last spring for his 80th birthday concerts, and right through the last time we saw him, teaching at his Carnegie Hall

Workshop in June 2001. We all feel the loss of a great artist and a great spokesman for culture and humanity.

Shumsky and Pressler

PS: In 1988 we had a wonderful opportunity to invite Menahem Pressler and Oscar Shumsky to tour with us - unfortunately too short a tour - in which they played a Fauré Sonata, we played either Debussy or Ravel String Quartet,

▽ In the control room with Rostropovich and DG producer Chris Alder

and together we played the Chausson Concerto for Violin, Piano and String Quartet. Five years later, we taped a radio program for St. Paul Sunday with Shumsky, which was wonderful because he had stopped performing for a while after the death of his wife Louise, and it brought him back to playing. His passing in the summer of 2000 left a gaping hole for all of us.

Schubert with Slava

PS: I could write a book on the week in 1990 we spent recording the Schubert Cello Quintet with Rostropovich. It was one of the highlights of our career to perform and record and eat meals and drink vodka with someone like Rostropovich. The inspiration was remarkable. I remember one story in particular which is worth mentioning.

We had finished the first movement in the morning and were invited to lunch by the mayor of the little town of Speyer, where we were recording. We had a big, heavy lunch. We went back to record the slow movement - one of the most glorious slow movements ever written - and it felt pretty awful. To hear playbacks, we had to go from the church to another building where the equipment was stored. It was a very cold day, the ground was covered with ice and snow, and Slava was holding on to my arm as we walked. I said, "I'm not sure how this is going to go - we're all so full from this lunch." And he said, "Well let's listen to it..." We listened to what we had just done, and after a minute or two he stopped and said, "You're right. We must take nap! Everybody take nap, come back tonight." So we all went and rested and came back that night. There was a street light outside the window and I

With Oscar Shumsky (center) and St. Paul Sunday host Bill McGlaughlin ▷

Photograph by Steve Barnett

could see the snow falling. And the quiet in this little town at night - whenever snow falls it creates a certain kind of quiet - felt just perfect for the setting of the slow movement. When I think of that movement I always imagine sitting in that church with Slava and looking out, seeing the snow.

Pressler recordings

DF: Menahem Pressler was our first collaborator who was an internationally recognized performer. But Menahem is not only a famous pianist and a great musician, he's also a great teacher and a close friend - and he's remained true to that role in our lives until this day. He still comes up with the most forceful, creative and constructive criticism of our playing, always bringing us to a higher level, and we were very fortunate to have him as one of our first collaborators in a recording project.

When DG approached us with the idea to record collaborations with piano, only one pianist seemed like the right choice. We had played the repertoire for piano and strings with Menahem far more than with any other pianist, and in many ways we learned how to play those pieces with him and from him. The recording sessions in '93 and '94, in New York for Dvorak and in Munich for Schumann, were pivotal musical experiences for us. They were important opportunities for us to document our relationship with this great musician, who had influenced us so profoundly. ☯

ED on Shumsky

Many string players and music lovers would acknowledge that the death of Oscar Shumsky signals the end of an era. But when speaking of such a unique musician, it is hard to define that era without the risk of pigeonholing him. True, he was an exemplar of a bygone romantic tradition of violin playing: the last of Leopold Auer's pupils, he had that sumptuous Russian sound, but also the elegance and rhythmic incisiveness of Fritz Kreisler, who was always his great violinistic inspiration. He left a personal stamp on everything he interpreted, and his musical voice could never be confused with that of any other great violinist. Strongly marked individuality was one of the chief characteristics of that slightly undefined, multi-faceted "era" of which we like to speak: all the greats sounded like themselves, and different from each other, without gimmicky attempts at originality or eccentricity artificially pumped up for the sake of public relations.

Chapter 8

The recording decade 1990-2000

International Management Group

DF: An important event took place in June 1989, when we signed a new management contract with IMG Artists in New York. Originally founded as an exclusive management by Charles Hamlen and Edna Landau, the company had grown under its new parent, International Management Group, into one of the most important artist agencies in the world. With the initial guidance of Edna and Charlie, the continuing dedication of our brilliant personal manager Elizabeth Sobol, and the constant attention to detail from IMG's dedicated staff, we are now able to navigate a complex schedule filled with major projects. We could not have survived, much less succeeded, without IMG's extraordinary work.

Photograph by Werner Neumeister; courtesy of Deutsche Grammophon

Beethoven in Badenweiler

I don't think that in 1991 we knew that we'd be recording the Beethovens soon, but probably some little bird was telling us that we'd better get ready. Our first chance to play the cycle in Europe was offered to us in the 1990-91 season by Klaus Lauer at the Hotel Römerbad. It was a grand occasion where our families, and in some cases extended families and friends from as far away as Denver, made the journey with us.

Beethoven and Shostakovich

PS: In early 1993 we inaugurated the first of two series at the 92nd St. Y in New York. One of the series combined a wide variety of works, ranging from Schubert to Sibelius and Berg. However, the series that really turned some heads was the one there in 1994 which combined late Beethoven and late Shostakovich.

Upon learning the late quartets of Shostakovich (we went more or less right to them after beginning our own study of the quartets with the 8th), we all perceived the similarities of musical language between these two great composers. In addition, they were two of history's most oppressed artists: Beethoven by his deafness, and Shostakovich by the politics of his country. We also presented a similar series in Aspen in the summer of 1994, which is when we began to record Shostakovich, so in many ways the recordings were born from the idea of this series.

The release list for the decade

In reviewing the archival materials for this period, we were astonished to see the continuity of our recording life over the past ten years. In this chapter we'll look at the quartet's life from that perspective.

1. **1990** Prokofiev quartets and violin duo
2. **1991** Mozart flute quartets with Carol Wincenc
3. **1992** American Originals (Ives and Barber)
4. **1992** Schubert cello quintet with Mstislav Rostropovich
5. **1994** American Contemporaries (Harbison, Wernick, Schuller)
6. **1994** Dvorak piano quintet and quartet with Menahem Pressler
7. **1994** Six Mozart quartets dedicated to Haydn
8. **1994** Barber "Dover Beach" with Thomas Hampson
9. **1995** Webern complete works for string quartet
10. **1995** Schumann piano quintet and quartet with Menahem Pressler
11. **1997** Beethoven quartets
12. **1998** Schubert A minor quartet and Quartettsatz
13. **1998** Rorem Quartet and Meyer Quintet
14. **1999** Mozart and Brahms clarinet quintets with David Shifrin
15. **2000** Shostakovich

New music recordings

In the early 90's we recorded some music that may have been unfamiliar to many listeners. Sometimes, when performers become well-known enough, listeners will trust them and listen to something new. DG must have felt confident enough about our popularity at this point to begin having us record some pretty tough stuff.

DF: We began with the Prokofiev Quartets and Sonata for Two Violins, beautiful works not played nearly often enough. Especially the 1st quartet, which is a deeply-felt and challenging piece.

LD: The American Originals record was next. Being Americans, I guess, we felt very natural with Ives, as crazy and wild as some of it is. Also, people in other countries like us to bring Ives and Barber and other American music to play for them. I guess they assume they're getting an authentic interpretation!

It was great fun making that record because we could finally step back from the Ives Quartets and hear how they sounded from outside. What an unbelievable imagination he had, and what courage to let it run so freely almost a hundred years ago. And this project gave us the chance to record the great Barber Adagio, a timeless masterpiece that's always in our repertoire. The record got a Grammy in '94 for Best Chamber Music Performance.

DF: I remember that, all right. Our daughter Lilian was born on Friday, we played a concert at the 92nd Y on the weekend, and the Grammy came the following Tuesday. What a week! The house was filled with flowers and champagne....

ED: And after that we pulled some pieces out of the hat that we had learned over the previous five years, all written for us - the quartets of Gunther Schuller, John Harbison, and Richard Wernick - and made a kind of sequel to the Originals record: American Contemporaries, which came out in 1994.

DG's complete Webern project was under the direction of Pierre Boulez. We recorded all the music for string quartet, which included a couple of pieces for string trio as well - some of which we had never played before. We had only played a few pieces of Webern in concert and we believed in them very strongly, but DG unearthed everything that Webern had written for strings. I'm proud of that recording, I think it came out very well. It was nominated for a Grammy.

DF: I finally got to record my once-dreaded Fünf Stücke, which now seemed like child's play next to Webern's String Trio, probably the most complicated piece we've ever had to put together, right down to the page turns.

Intensive preparation

LD: One thing that was very important in our early years, for which we're indebted to Melvin Kaplan, is that he arranged for us to perform the Beethoven cycle at his Mozart Festival in Vermont. The Beethoven cycle is the centerpiece of the string quartet repertoire, and it was crucial for us to begin learning all the quartets as soon as possible and to be able to start performing complete cycles. Those pieces are the greatest teachers.

We've been playing the complete cycle for 21 of our 25 years. I realize that many other groups don't learn the complete cycle that early in their careers, because it's a huge commitment. But on the other hand, I think that the early start gave us one of our strengths.

PS: We often play the quartets in chronological order, and not just for the sake of being different. I think that this idea came out of our experience of doing the Bartok cycle chronologically - the sense of not only the musical journey, but the life journey of the composer through his music. You really go through Beethoven's life, especially because the late quartets are some of the last pieces he wrote.

Recording Beethoven

ED: In 1994 our main focus became the recording of the Beethoven cycle, which we began at the American Academy of Arts and Letters in New York. Since we had a lot of experience performing the cycle in concentrated periods of time (six concerts in eight days), we believed

1988-89 Thirteenth Season

September	European tour: 2 concerts, Wigmore Hall. Tour of Germany, 6 cities plus recording sessions of Mozart "Haydn" Quartets, Cologne First concert, BASF, Ludwigshafen, Germany
October	Carnegie Hall debut, Bartok marathon Release of the Bartok Quartets
November	Kennedy Center with Menahem Pressler
December	Recording sessions for Schubert G major, Beethoven Op. 135, NY
January	Premiere of Richard Danielpour's Quintet, with pianist Ken Noda, at Alice Tully Hall
February	First appearance on Lincoln Center's Great Performers Series
March	European tour, Germany and Switzerland, 14 cities
May	Quartet records laser disc of Mozart string quintets with violist Kim Kashkashian, for Teldec
June	Quartet signs exclusive management contract with IMG (International Management Group), NY
July	Mostly Mozart, Lincoln Center, NY, with Alicia de Larrocha

1989-90 Fourteenth Season

October	Gramophone Awards for Best Chamber Music Recording, and Record of the Year for the Bartok quartets
November	European tour: Utrecht, Rome, Naples, Caserta, Florence, Valencia, Geneva, Bern, Paris
February	Two Grammy Awards: for Best Chamber Music Performance, and for Best Classical Album, for the complete Bartok Quartets Metropolitan Museum of Art, late Schubert and late Beethoven. Schubert Quintet with Bernard Greenhouse
March	European tour: Neumarkt, Mannheim, Strasbourg, Bonn, Amsterdam, Hamburg, Lübeck, Basel, Vevey, Zurich, Luxembourg, London, Leeds
May	Recording sessions for Mozart Flute Quartets with Carol Wincenc, NY
July	European tour: Pollensa, Montpellier, Hitzacker, Copenhagen, Passau, Salzburg, Weimar

1990-91 Fifteenth Season

September	Release of the recording of Prokofiev Quartets and the Sonata for Two Violins

at first that we could attempt a concentrated timetable for our recording project. We predicted when we started in early 1994 that we would finish the project in 13 months. That turned out to be unrealistic, because our musical discoveries during the recording process caused us to make a major reassessment of our interpretations.

Questions arose from Beethoven's own metronome indications for the early and middle quartets, which he added years after he composed them, when the metronome was invented. We felt an obligation to fully explore those markings, to see what they revealed about how Beethoven heard the music in his head, and to decide how many of them were practical. As expected, Beethoven's indications worked for some movements and not for others. We went back and re-recorded a good portion of the cycle, so in fact the recording took twice as much time as we thought, lasting from early '94 to the spring of '96. The cycle was released in 1997.

Life goes on in spite of recording

DF: I recall feeling during those years as if we never really left the studio, or went home. Many times, even on the day of returning home from a tour, we'd trek up to the American Academy at 155th street, grab some Cuban-Chinese food, and record another movement or two.

We did manage to continue a heavy concert schedule, though. We played Bartok Marathons in London, Sydney, Turin, New York's Avery Fisher Hall and at Tanglewood in 1995. Why, I don't know, now that I look back. The Beethovens should have been enough to keep in our fingers. There's something about being asked....

PS: But at least we played the Beethovens again at Badenweiler. We couldn't quite believe that Klaus wanted us to repeat the cycle after only a few seasons,

but the first experience had been so positive, we somehow all felt the need to repeat it. And all the families came again (many of them bigger!) and we played and partied as before.

LD: In '95 we also premiered two great new pieces: Edgar Meyer's Bass Quintet, which we played together with him, and a fantastic quartet by Ned Rorem. We later recorded the two together.

The quartets of Shostakovich

DF: All this overlaps with the beginning of our Shostakovich project. Like with the Bartok quartets years earlier, it was Phil who somehow in the midst of all this insanity found the time and focus to sit and listen to all 15 of them. He became more and more enthusiastic and eventually persuaded us to commit to performing the entire cycle, though the idea to record came afterwards.

ED: Historical context becomes very important when listening to Shostakovich's music because of what was going on in the Soviet Union, because of the various waves of falling in and out of favor that Shostakovich experienced vis-à-vis the cultural commissars. Before he ever wrote a string quartet, the premiere of his opera Lady Macbeth resulted in a dire warning in Pravda, which some people believe was ghost-written by Stalin. But Shostakovich came back into favor, and then again in the late 40s fell out of favor.

The string quartets represent a very interesting part of his output because, though he still had to be careful when writing them, he knew they weren't being scrutinized to quite the same extent as his symphonic music or film scores or operas, because those would tend to be disseminated to a much larger audience than quartets. Nevertheless, we feel that he wrote in an encoded musical language which employed many elements, such as sardonic humor - music that seems happy on the surface but actually isn't if you delve more deeply.

Shostakovich started writing quartets later in his career than many other writers of great string quartets - Bartok, like Beethoven, produced his first quartet when he was 27. Shostakovich wrote his first quartet after he wrote his famous Fifth Symphony. The Second Quartet was written during World War II, around the same time as the Seventh Symphony. In 1960, after he visited Dresden and saw the horrific effects of the fire-bombing, he wrote the Eighth

European tour: Cremona, Turin, Brussels, Aalst, Montreux, Ludwigsburg, Toulouse, Leuwen, Weiden, Landshut. Collaborations with soprano Barbara Hendricks

December   Concert and **recording of the Schubert Quintet** with Rostropovich, BASF, Ludwigshafen

January   Appearance at Carnegie Hall, Russian program, with Yefim Bronfman, Gary Hoffman and Kim Kashkashian

March   First Beethoven Cycle at the Hotel Römerbad in Badenweiler, Germany

April   Premiere of **Richard Wernick's String Quartet**, Philadelphia Chamber Music Society

May   Third tour of Japan. 2 Mozart programs broadcast on the Japanese television network NHK
            Second tour of Australia
            First appearance in **Taiwan**, Taipei Cultural Center, with Wu Han, pianist

1991-92 Sixteenth Season

September   Release of the **Mozart Flute Quartets** with Carol Wincenc
October   Beginning of a Mozart series at the Metropolitan Museum of Art, NY
November   European tour: Florence, Munich, Salzburg, Graz
December   First appearance at **London's Royal Festival Hall**, Mozart 200th anniversary concert
February   Philip Setzer acquires a **Lupot** violin
May   Concerto appearances with the **Omaha Symphony**, Omaha, Nebraska
June   European festival tour: Schubertiade, Feldkirch, Austria; Divonne, Tours and Dijon France

1992-93 Seventeenth Season

September   European festival tour: Berlin, Helsinki, Lucerne, Ascona, Turin, Montreux
November 28 **Lawrence Dutton and Elizabeth Lim-Dutton's son, Luke, is born**
October   Release of "American Originals" quartets by Samuel Barber and Charles Ives
January   First of two series at the 92nd St. Y, NY. Works of Schubert, combined with Berg, Rihm, Sibelius, Dvorak
May   Residency at the Evian Festival as quartet competition judges.

The quartet apears in the "The Noise of Time ", a collaboration with the theatrical company Complicité. The ▷ performance is a 90-minute portrait, in words, images, and music, of composer Dmitri Shostakovich, and includes an uninterrupted performance of Shostakovich's 15th and final quartet.

Quartet, a starkly pessimistic work dedicated to the victims of fascism and war. But even here we feel that there is a subtext. In this case it is his despair over having recently joined the Communist Party. Unlike some other people, we feel that he was extremely conflicted about his role in Soviet cultural life and about what the Communist Party was doing. And he was at the brink of suicide. He wrote to a friend and said to think of the Eighth Quartet as his epitaph. The music functions on a very personal level also because Shostakovich incorporated his own initials (DSCH) as the first four notes of the quartet, and included many references to his earlier works. So, even though the quartet purports to be about the major events of the mid-century, it is also about the anguish and struggle of a creative artist who was constantly being manipulated by the state, and expresses his despair over having joined the Communist Party.

Another example is the Sixth Quartet, which he wrote when he turned 50. It was supposed to be a sort of 50th birthday present to himself, which he was encouraged to write by the League of Soviet Composers. And on the surface it's a pretty cheerful work (except for the slow movement), but there is also a lot of anguish beneath the surface. We feel that anguish throughout most of his works.

The Shostakovich recordings

LD: We spent three years of our lives really focusing on the Beethoven quartets, performing the cycle as we were recording. In our programming we started to combine late Beethoven with late Shostakovich. Although we were already committed to record the Beethoven Quartets in 1994 we decided to record Shostakovich as well. The Aspen Music Festival had just built a magnificent new hall, Harris Concert Hall, and we felt it would be the perfect setting. We talked to DG about the possibility of recording the Shostakovich quartets there, live. We felt that having the audience present was necessary for the tension of those

Photograph by Joan Marcus

Performances of Tchaikovsky "Souvenir de Florence" and Arensky
Quartet with Rostropovich

June   Beethoven cycle, Tivoli Festival, Copenhagen

1993-94 Eighteenth Season

September   David Finckel acquires a **Samuel Zygmuntowicz cello** (1993,
                      Brooklyn, NY), a copy of the "Duport" Stradivarius (commissioned by DF)
                      Beginning of Beethoven cycle for BASF, Ludwigshafen, Germany

November   Premiere of **Wolfgang Rihm's 9th Quartet**, commissioned by Klaus
                      Lauer, at the Hotel Römerbad
                      Concerto appearances with the **Hartford Symphony**, Connecticut

December   Recording of **Barber's "Dover Beach"** with Thomas Hampson

February   The quartet begins recording the complete **Beethoven Quartets**
                      Second series at the 92nd St. Y. (late Beethoven and Shostakovich)
                      Concerto appearances with the **Richmond Symphony**, Virginia

February 25   **Wu Han and David Finckel's daughter, Lilian, is born**

February 28   Quartet receives **Grammy** for Best Chamber Music Performance for
                      the recording "American Originals" (Barber and Ives)

March 16   **Roberta Cooper and Eugene Drucker's son, Julian, is born**
                      Release of **Mozart's Six Quartets** dedicated to Haydn
                      Release of **Dvorak piano quartet and piano quintet**, with pianist
                      Menahem Pressler (the recording was subsequently nominated for a
                      Grammy)

April   Release of recording entitled **"American Contemporaries"**. Quartets
                      by **John Harbison, Richard Wernick,** and **Gunther Schuller**

May   Quartet receives the University Medal from the University of Hartford

July   Beginning of **Shostakovich recordings** at the Aspen Music Festival
                      (late quartets)

1994-95 Nineteenth Season

September   Premiere of **Paul Epstein's String Quartet**, South Mountain Concerts,
                      Pittsfield, Massachussetts

October   Carnegie Hall, with Menahem Pressler

November   Release of **Barber's "Dover Beach"** with Thomas Hampson

March   Premiere of **Edgar Meyer's Quintet** for string quartet and bass, Chicago

May   **Honorary Doctorates** from Middlebury College, Vermont

June   Bartok Marathons in London and Sydney (third Australian tour)
                      First concerts in **New Zealand**

The late Isaac Stern with the cast of "The Noise of Time". Left to right: ED, DF, Stern, PS, Richard Katz (seated), Toby Sedgwick, LD, Antonio Gil Martinez, Tim McMullan

pieces, that it would help the performances for us to feel that people were holding their collective breath, rather than playing to an empty hall. It was really a risk, an experiment, and it was very stressful to do it, but in the end it went extremely well. Of course we were committed through the next two years to record our Beethoven cycle, but after listening to those first Shostakovich performances we decided that we also wanted to complete that cycle. So the next big step in our career, which brings us close to the present, was our involvement with Shostakovich - and this goes in three parts: finishing the recordings at Aspen, the performances of the complete cycle in New York and London, and our collaboration with Simon McBurney and Complicité in the theater piece called "The Noise of Time."

The Noise of Time

PS: When I look back at the repertoire we've done, it really has been quite organic, in the sense of our becoming interested in weaving the life of Bartok through the Bartok cycle, in weaving the life of Beethoven through the Beethoven cycle, and then the same again with Shostakovich. Shostakovich quartets and theater was an idea that we discussed long ago, especially because of the many questions surrounding the life of Shostakovich.

We had become aware of a remarkable dramatic tension in the air during performances of the Shostakovich string quartets, as though they were already theater pieces, with Shostakovich's controversial and tortured life as the dramatic center. I originally thought of a theatrical setting for the whole cycle of 15 quartets (sometimes even good ideas are just too big!). Later, when it was decided that we should focus on one quartet, I was sure that it should be the

△ A lighting cue excerpt from "The Noise of Time"

15th. It is his final quartet and one of his last compositions, a haunting work of remembrance. Its structure is also most unusual - six slow movements played without pause.

There's another interesting connection from our experience with Rostropovich. We felt close second-hand contact with Shostakovich through Rostropovich, through the stories that he told us. During the time that we recorded the Schubert Quintet together we prodded him for stories about Shostakovich and Prokofiev. His insights on Shostakovich reinforced our sense that Shostakovich was the right person about whom to make this theater piece. Happily, it's been a wonderful collaboration with Simon McBurney and the company, and we've now performed the work in New York, London and Berlin, and will be doing it in a number of places around the world. It was also filmed for television in London by the BBC. The result is an example of what can be accomplished in terms of developing an idea that comes from the right place. We owe a great deal to Jane Moss of Lincoln Center for producing The Noise of Time, and of course, to Simon for creating and directing it.

The Emerson and String Theory

ED: In May 1999 and April 2000, at the Guggenheim Museum, we collaborated with the well-known physicist Brian Greene in a special presentation called

July Bartok Marathon at Tanglewood

1995-96 Twentieth Season

September Bartok Marathon in Turin, Italy

October Premiere of **Ned Rorem's Quartet No. 4**, South Mountain Concerts, Pittsfield, Massachussetts

Release of the **Schumann Piano Quartet and Quintet** with Menahem Pressler

November Second Beethoven cycle at the Hotel Römerbad

December Bartok Marathon, Avery Fisher Hall, NY

January Release of **Webern's complete works for string quartet**

February Premiere of **Curt Cacioppo's quartet "Monsterslayer"**, Philadelphia Chamber Music Society

June First concerts in **Israel**. First participation in **Isaac Stern Chamber Music Encounters** in Jerusalem

July 10 **Lawrence Dutton and Elizabeth Lim-Dutton's second son, Jesse, is born**

1996-97 Twenty-first Season

September Beethoven cycle in **Saitama**, Japan

October NY premiere of Meyer Quintet, Chamber Music Society of Lincoln Center.

January Beginning of a two-season series at Alice Tully Hall, Lincoln Center, NY, "Beethoven and the 20th Century"

European tour: Amsterdam, the Hague, Florence, Genoa, Bologna, Dresden, Ludwigshafen, Münster

February Three-concert series in Montreal featuring works of Brahms and Schubert

March Release of the complete **Beethoven Quartets**

May Quartet participates for the first time in the **Isaac Stern Chamber Music Workshop** at Carnegie Hall, NY

1997-98 Twenty-second Season

October **Orchestra Hall**, Chicago

February **Grammy** award for Best Chamber Music Performance for the Beethoven Quartets.

March Shostakovich series at the Hotel Römerbad, with Yefim Bronfman and Rosemary Hardy

April Quartet receives **National Public Radio** award for the Beethoven Quartets

Release of the **Meyer-Rorem** recording

July Recording sessions for the **middle quartets of Shostakovich** in Aspen

1998-99 Twenty-third Season

September European tour: Berlin Festival, Paris; concerto appearances with Orchestra of the Rheinland-Pfalz in Frankfurt (Alte Oper), Ludwigshafen and Mainz

December Premiere of **Ellen Taaffe Zwilich's Quartet No. 2** at Carnegie Hall

February European tour: Munich, Amsterdam, Ghent, Vienna (with André Previn), London, Dijon

March Release of **Mozart and Brahms Clarinet Quintets** with David Shifrin

May First performance of **'Strings and Strings'**, a multi-media collaboration with physicist Brian Greene, at the Guggenheim Museum in NY

Sixth tour of Japan

July Recording sessions for the **early quartets of Shostakovich** in Aspen

1999-2000 Twenty-fourth Season

December Musical America names the quartet **Ensemble of the Year**

January Philip Setzer acquires a **Samuel Zygmuntowicz violin** (1999, Brooklyn, NY, a copy of Oscar Shumsky's "Rode" Stradivarius, commissioned by PS)

Release of complete **Shostakovich Quartets**

February First **Shostakovich cycle** at Lincoln Center

March World premiere performances of **"The Noise of Time"**, a collaboration between the Emerson Quartet and London-based theater company Complicité, Simon McBurney, director. Presented by Lincoln Center's "New Visions" series, at the John Jay Theater, NY

May Shostakovich cycle in London, at the Wigmore Hall and Barbican Centre

June Fourth tour to Australia and and second to New Zealand

2000-01 Twenty-fifth Season

October Tour: Iowa City (Shostakovich series), Minneapolis

Carnegie Hall as guests on Maurizio Pollini's "Perspectives" series

December European tour: Paris (series at the Louvré), Cologne, Berlin, Bonn

February First performances in **Hong Kong** and **Singapore**.

Two **Grammy** awards: for Best Chamber Music Performance, and Best Classical Album. The album also won the **Record Academy Prize**,

Photograph by Roger Mastroianni; courtesy of the Cleveland Orchestra

"Strings and Strings". Brian outlined the history of physics from Newton through Einstein, quantum mechanics and beyond, to current attempts to find a grand unifying theory that will bridge the gap between general relativity and quantum mechanics.

Brian is a charismatic speaker and author, capable of making scientific concepts comprehensible and exciting for a lay audience. He and I worked closely together to select eight or ten pieces of music that would either illustrate the concepts he was explaining or would demonstrate parallels between scientific and musical history. Webern's break with tonality mirrored Einstein's radical departure from classical physics; Bach fugues transcribed by Mozart evoked the clockwork universe envisioned by Newton. The muted frenzy of the third movement of Berg's "Lyric Suite" illustrated the quivering loops of energy in the sub-microscopic realm of string theory, Brian Greene's principal area of research. The program, filmed for CNN and ABC's Nightline, was dedicated to the memory of Brian's father and my father-in-law, who were lifelong friends. ∘ʼ

	and the **Gramophone Award** for Best Chamber Music Recording. 2nd concert at Carnegie Hall as guests on Maurizio Pollini's "Perspectives" series
March	Performances at Boston's Symphony Hall and Washington's Kennedy Center with Isaac Stern as part of his 80th birthday celebration, including premiere of **William Bolcom's Quintet**, with pianists Jonathan Biss and Yefim Bronfman
July	Eleven performances of "The Noise of Time" at the Barbican Centre

2001-02 Twenty-sixth Season

September 16	Free performance, "A Concert of Healing and Remembrance", at Avery Fisher Hall, Lincoln Center
September	Appearances as soloists with the Cleveland Orchestra, Christoph von Dohnányi, conductor, in the US premiere of Wolfgang Rihm's "Dithyrambe" for quartet and orchestra, Severance Hall, Cleveland
	3 performances of "The Noise of Time" at the Berlin Festival
	Release of "The Haydn Project"
October	2 performances of "The Noise of Time" at the Krannert Center in Urbana, Illinois
	6 performances of "The Noise of Time" at the John Jay Theater in NY
	4 performances of "The Noise of Time" at the Massachusetts International Arts Festival
November	25th Anniversary programs at London's South Bank Center
January	Rihm Concerto with the Cleveland Orchestra, Symphony Hall, Boston, and Carnegie Hall, NY
	25th Anniversary series begins at Lincoln Center, Haydn program, with Beethoven and Bartok programs in February and March
April	Tour with the Kalichstein-Laredo-Robinson Trio, celebrating both ensembles' 25th year anniversaries
April	European tour: Basel, Milan, Turin, Vevey, Antwerp, Münster, London, Birmingham, Bologna, Amsterdam, Bilbao, Madrid, Paris
June	First appearances at the Ojai Festival, Calirformia
	First tour to South America

Chapter 9

The 25th Anniversary Season

PS, ED, LD, DF: Our 25th season was actually 2000-01. So we could say that in 2001-2 we are celebrating *having made it through 25 seasons* (this is attributable in a large way to the miracles worked for us by our amazing travel agent, Diana Howard). For the occasion of this anniversary season we thought carefully about our repertoire. We wanted not only to represent our interests and strengths, but to celebrate the string quartet in general. This could be accomplished, on both accounts, by playing the music of a wide variety of composers, as we have been doing for our entire career. But we opted for a leaner approach which would attempt to define the art of the string quartet, while at the same time allowing us to perform some of our favorite works.

Haydn, the undisputed "father" of the quartet, gave us an invaluable repertoire which has shown every composer since the possibilities of the string quartet. Beethoven, as we all know, elevated the art form to new heights, and his "Razumovsky" quartets ushered in a new dimension of grand, heroic scale. In the 20th century, Bartok took up in many ways where Beethoven left off, expanding quartet technique to include previously unimagined colors, rhythms, counterpoint, and even ethnic flavor.

We have no doubt that our anniversary series will tax our abilities and enrich us through the challenge. We hope, as always, that the result of our efforts is worthy of the attention and faith that our public so generously affords us.

The 25th Anniversary Concerts

Program I
The Haydn Project

Quartet in F minor, Op. 20, No. 5
Quartet in Eb major "The Joke", Op. 33, No. 2
Intermission
Quartet in D major "The Lark", Op. 64, No. 5
Quartet in G minor "Rider", Op. 74, No. 3
Intermission
Quartet in D minor "Fifths", Op. 76, No. 2
Quartet in G major, Op. 77, No. 1

Program II
Beethoven: the "Razumovsky" Quartets

Quartet in F major, Op. 59, No. 1
Quartet in E minor, Op. 59, No. 2
Intermission
Quartet in C major, Op. 59, No. 3

Program III
The Bartok Marathon

Quartet No. 1, (1908)
Quartet No. 2 (1915)
Intermission
Quartet No. 3 (1927)
Quartet No. 4 (1928)
Intermission
Quartet No. 5 (1934)
Quartet No. 6 (1939)

Piano	Viola	Winds	Violin	Voice
Menahem Pressler	Walter Trampler	Michael Parloff	Oscar Shumsky	Thomas Hampson
Jean-Bernard	Robert Vernon	Carol Wincenc	Joseph Silverstein	Lucy Shelton
Pommier	Eric Shumsky	David Shifrin	Isaac Stern	Jan DeGaetani
Rudolf Firkusny	Michael Tree	Loren Kitt	Joshua Bell	Rosemary Hardy
Lilian Kallir	Josef Suk	Ransom Wilson	Elizabeth Lim Dutton	Barbara Hendricks
Claude Frank	Scott Nickrenz	Charles Neidich	James Buswell	Elizabeth Mannion
Gilbert Kalish	Paul Neubauer	Eduard Brunner	Ani Kavafian	Betsy Norden
Ken Noda	Masao Kawasaki	Heinz Holliger		Leslie Guinn
Charles Wadsworth	Heiichiro Ohyama	Robert Routch		Charles Bressler
Richard Goode	Ynez Lynch	Gervase de Peyer		Bethany Beardslee
Lee Luvisi	Jorge Mester	Paula Robison		David Gordon
David Golub	Burton Fine	Richard Stoltzman		
Yefim Bronfman	Jaime Laredo	Sara Stern		
Jonathan Biss	Abraham Skernick	Franklin Cohen		
Wu Han	Donald McGinnes	Paul Meyer		
Leon Fleisher	Yuri Bashmet	Milan Turkovich		
Misha Dichter	Kim Kashkashian	Charles Russo		
Anne Koscielny	Steven Tenenbom			
Joseph Kalichstein				
André Previn				
Emanuel Ax				
Ruth Laredo				
Alicia DeLarrocha				
Irma Vallecillo				
Stephen Hough				
Oleg Maisenberg				
Jean-Yves Thibaudet				
Lambert Orkis				
Zoltan Kocsis				
Maria Joao Pires				
Gerhard Oppitz				
Cynthia Siebert				
Harriet Wingreen				

Collaborators

Bass	Cello
Tim Cobb	Anner Bylsma
Edgar Meyer	Nathaniel Rosen
Eugene Levinson	Carter Brey
Bruce Bransby	Gary Hoffman
Donald Palma	Antonio Meneses
	Laurence Lesser
	Bernard Greenhouse
	Gustav Rivinius
String quartets	Jules Eskin
	Denis Brott
Guarneri	Frederick Zlotkin
St. Lawrence	Mstislav Rostropovich
Primavera	Lynn Harrell
Mendelssohn	Hakuro Mori
Pro Arte	Antonio Lysy
	Fortunato Arico
	Peter Wiley
	Fred Sherry
	Sharon Robinson
	Leslie Parnas
	Eric Wilson
	Roberta Cooper
	Colin Carr
	Frans Helmerson

The opportunity to work with gifted guest artists has been one of the largest components of our musical education, both as individuals and as an ensemble. No matter how resourceful and creative four people may be, we are still four people, and when we look at our list of past collaborators, not to mention our teachers and coaches, we realize that our musicianship is really an amalgam of influences. When we are fortunate enough to be working with artists such as those on our list, we never ask them to play a piece our way – we seek to try their tempi, imitate their sound, and gain their perspective. Those influences have all become a part of our musical DNA.

It's not really possible here, although it would be fun, to talk in depth about every musician who has crossed our path. What we'd like to say to all of them is a heartfelt thanks for sharing the stage, and their artistry, with us. And for those who have departed, we assure them that we'll always carry cherished pieces of their musicianship with us.

Editor's note: the following list was compiled from the Emerson's date books. Please forgive us for any omitted names.

NED ROREM

For The Emerson Quartet   11 Sept. 01

In an increasingly one-dimensional world, truly good music has come to be a cry in the wilderness. Yet this cry is forceful by its very rarity, and never has it sounded more thrilling than through the Emerson String Quartet. These four young players, alone and together, are ~~responsible~~ dedicated, polished, and virtuosically inspired.

Ours is the only period in history wherein the performance of music of the past takes precedence over music of the present. Again the Emerson is a resposible exception: for 25 years they have championed living composers of every language. Speaking for myself, their creation of my Fourth Quartet was one of my happiest experiences; they played at the same speed as the blood flowing through my veins.

The Emerson is technically the best, and sociologically the most interesting, string-quartet in America today.

Ned Rorem

EDGAR MEYER ROREM · String Quartet No. 4
MEYER · Quintet EMERSON STRING QUARTET

– WORLD PREMIERE RECORDINGS –

Having a chance to work with the Emersons was a musical coming of age for me. I will always remember the thrill of the first rehearsal in Larry's apartment hearing sounds up close that I had only heard from afar or imagined. That experience immediately confirmed for me that this group is certainly the prototype when it comes to four rich and interesting personalities coming together to create something much bigger than the sum of the parts.

Happy Anniversary gentlemen, and I hope for myself that I am able to enjoy many more years of the Emerson Quartet.

Edgar Meyer

25 years of the Emerson Quartet.

I am sitting looking out on my mother's garden in Cambridge, not Mass but UK. It is an autumn afternoon. Thinking of the Emerson Quartet, the only thing that comes to mind is that they are marvellous. That does not sound like much of a birthday tribute, but let me try to explain. The dictionary defines this word as the capacity to 'astonish', 'surprise' and above all to '...excite wonder'. When Phil Setzer first asked me to collaborate on a work based on Shostakovitch's 15th Quartet, I was uncertain, skeptical even. How could you dramatize, that is to say make public, firstly a form which is so personal and secondly a piece which is so fragile. But when I first heard them play, all doubts were swept away. I was astonished, surprised and full of wonder; and not only because I realized that such a collaboration would be, could be possible and thrilling.It was, certainly, 'surprising' to discover that pieces I thought I knew well were offered up to me in a way that made it seem as if I had never heard them before; and 'astonishing' that, such was the delicacy and precision of performance, all of us in this hall of 1000 people imagined, indeed were convinced, they were playing for us each individually. However something else was 'marvellous' too. Another quality much harder to define and which I have observed with amazement and no small degree of envy in the two years I have had the privilege of working with them. This quality derives not only from the creativity of playing together over time. Nor from the creativity in the skill and attention they bring to every moment of every piece they offer us. It is a creativity that is more mysterious. It is the creativity of the 'sayer' as Ralph Waldo Emerson calls those who 'express'. He was referring to poets when he wrote that. And if a poet is, in Emerson's words, someone who '...stands among partial men for the complete man, and apprises us not of his wealth, but of the commonwealth', then this Quartet is made of poets. But the mystery is deeper. When they play it is as if there is nothing between you and the music. As if the musicians, curiously, are not there, but like glass in a window, allow you to see further than the room you are in. This is not a technique, though perhaps it is acquired over time. It comes from a humility and humanity that is out of kilter in these times of monstrous self-importance. A humility in the face of something that is much larger than the room of our small 'selves' and refers to what is mysterious and indefinable in this world. R.W. Emerson would have recognized this as 'Nature', I think. 'Our music, our poetry, our language itself are not satisfactions, but suggestions.' as he wrote in his essay, 'Nature'. It is this ability to 'suggest', with all the delicacy and tact that suggestion implies, which I find so remarkable and unique. Many musicians show extraordinary dedication, many have astonishing skill but when all that is subsumed into a unified voice of such selfless clarity and mystery, we feel hope in the possibility and capacity of human communication. This 'excites wonder'. It is indeed marvellous.

Simon McBurney
London Sept 2001

For the past 25 years the Emerson Quartet has represented with great distinction the musical domain that it has adopted as its own. It is a great pleasure to salute it now - on the anniversary of its founding - for its outstanding past achievements, and wish it continued creative vigor and fresh insights when sharing this great repertoire with true music lovers everywhere.

Menahem Pressler

It was some 20 years ago, in the early 1980's, that I first had the good fortune to work with the Emerson String Quartet. I was visiting professor of music history at Middlebury College in Vermont, and the Emerson Quartet was engaged as the quartet-in-residence for the autumn term. We did an extensive Mozart series together, including discarded movements (very interesting) as well as extensive sketches, extending to parts of whole movements which Mozart later rejected. And, of course, the Emersons played complete Mozart quartets as well, and I also had a chance to hear their soon-to-be-famous renditions of Beethoven quartets.

There were several things that immediately struck me about their performances. The most obvious one was the intense passion with which they played everything. The second was their sheer technical perfection; they had rehearsed everything with great attention to details The third was the fact that the two violins changed places, frequently, giving us a real sense of democracy. I thought they were a remarkable ensemble and would soon become world-famous. At that time I had barely heard their Haydn, but now, fortunately, we have a generous selection of CD's with seven representative quartets from opus 20 (1777) to opus 77 (1799). They devote the same intense study and passion to Haydn as to their other performances, and I salute their quarter of a century together! Continuez comme ça!

H. C. Robbins Landon
Domaine de Foncoussières
June 2001

It stands to reason that a great quartet requires four very strong players, but the Emersons go far beyond that! Each of them has a highly developed individual musical voice and each is a wonderful soloist. So the creative energy that drives Gene, Phil, Larry and David to speak as one voice must be very powerful indeed, and possibly it accounts for the larger-than-life musical statements they make. Ultimately, though, that unified voice, the ineffable opulence of their sound, the cutting intensity, the exquisite delicacy - all surpass common understanding. They make their statements with an inevitable logic and clarity, and force you to think about what you are hearing, to ponder it for days to come, and even to think back on it over time - even if you can't imagine how they do it. The Emerson Quartet has been in its prime for many years, giving indelible performances!

A cultural episode like the Emerson Quartet occurs rarely, and I feel lucky to be a contemporary who has had the opportunity to hear them throughout their stunning twenty-five year history.

Norma Hurlburt
Executive Director, Chamber Music
Society of Lincoln Center

The relationship between artist and manager is a complex and wondrous thing. When the artist is the four members of the Emerson String Quartet, with their four strong and distinctive personalities, the complexities and wondrousness increase by geometric proportions. At times, moving the Quartet toward a consensus can seem like harnessing the energy of four wild horses, each with his own personal destination. Sitting in a meeting with them at times feels like the physical manifestation of a Carter String Quartet: four different, seemingly unrelated voices speaking simultaneously and yet, in the end, achieving cohesion and meaningful unity. E-mail responses to a simple business question highlight their personal styles: the poetic Phil responding with the brief clarity of haiku or the summation of passionate lyricism; the thoughtful Gene turning a question of tour routing into a philosophical discussion; the practical Larry honing in on a target with unerring precision; the elusive and brilliant David mysteriously absent from the discussion and then swooping down at the last moment with an insight that transforms the discussion. Working with this type of energy is both supremely challenging and supremely gratifying, a form of professional alchemy. Of course, ultimately, the greatest alchemy is what the Emersons achieve onstage: through the white heat of the fires of their collective intelligence, passion and compassion, they forge their extraordinary individual personalities into one voice, giving expression to some of the most beautiful music ever written. On this day in September, one week after the attack on our beloved New York City, home of the Emerson String Quartet, I feel more strongly than ever that what these four alchemists produce is the most precious, the most exquisite and the most powerful substance on our fragile earth.

Elizabeth Sobol
IMG Artists

The art of great string quartet playing involves the successful integration of many diverse and complicating factors: personality differences, depth of musical involvement, technical finesse and the ability to communicate. The members of the Emerson Quartet both as individuals and as a group possess all of these attributes and more. They are wonderful human beings as well. The Naumburg Foundation is very proud of their quarter-century of accomplishments. Here is to twenty-five more!

Robert and Lucy Mann

25 YEARS is a long time for any relationship and Deutsche Grammophon is proud to have accompanied and documented this artistic partnership for most of this period.

The recordings we have made testify to the unique quality of the Emerson String Quartet and include many Grammy award-winning releases ranging from 'mainstream' repertoire such as Beethoven, Bartok, Shostakovich and Haydn to Webern and modern American composers.

What the recordings do not tell you is that these are four really nice guys. And while this fact is not necessarily an essential part of a successful artistic enterprise it is a reason, coupled with the quartet's undimmed and sheer pleasure in playing, why I am delighted for both musical and personal reasons that we will continue recording with the ESQ for the next five years and hopefully beyond.

Chris Alder
Executive Producer, Deutsche Grammophon

How do we thank the group that invested countless hours helping us decipher the voices of Beethoven, Bartok, Tchaikovsky, Berg, Schoenberg, Mozart, and Debussy? The group that taught us how to listen. That welcomed us into their busy lives in New York. The group that counseled us when we argued, that encouraged us when frustration took hold. That celebrated with us. The group that showed us the joy in quartet life.

The Emerson players were not only our teachers or colleagues. They became our family, in a city where we had none. They were a source of inexhaustible energy and optimism; a well of inspiration that was always full and always available.

Their influence on our group is profound. Not a week goes by without one of us making reference to them. "That phrase needs more articulation - like the Emerson"; "That tour schedule sounds impossible...Ah, come on, it is nothing like the Emerson's"; "Who do you think we should get to help us with that recording? Let's call the Emerson"; "I wonder what restaurant will be open late, after the concert. Ask the Emerson."

It is a great pleasure to join in celebrating this special anniversary. Cheers!

The St. Lawrence String Quartet

HAPPY BIRTHDAY: There are certain people who come into your life where, when asked to recollect when or where or how you met them, you cannot remember. They have such a pervasive claim on your heart, and such indisputable presence in your spirit, that you cannot recall life before their arrival and a future departure is unimaginable and unthinkable. For me, the Emerson String Quartet, as individuals, as a quartet, as dearest friends, as one of the world's greatest chamber ensembles, is and always will be at the center of what is most important to me. And it is one of my great blessings that they are, in reality, always there for me - at a dinner table in my home, in my car as I listen to their CDs; in Alice Tully Hall at Lincoln Center, during a Great Performers season; in Avery Fisher Hall as part of the Mostly Mozart Festival; and in theater spaces around the world with our ground-breaking theatrical collaboration The Noise of Time. I send them all my love and congratulations on their 25th Anniversary with the strong proviso and observation that they are only at the beginning.

Much love,
Jane S. Moss
Vice President for Programming
Lincoln Center for the Performing Arts

THE EMERSON QUARTET. Aside from the unchallenged instrumental mastery of each of its members, it strikes me that the reason the Emerson Quartet has mattered so much over this last quarter century is its remarkable ability to hold together a powerful collection of opposing forces - fierce energy, directed by high intelligence - total dedication leavened by a wicked sense of humor - a profound love and respect for the monuments of the past, coupled with an explorer_s sense of delight in discovery. I suspect that this delight is the spark which ignites their fire.

Long live the Emerson! Happy 25th! Here's to 25 more and 50 beyond that!

Bill McGlaughlin

The Emerson Quartet is celebrating its 25th Anniversary. 25 years together is a long time. 25 successful years together is even more remarkable and 25 years of being the best there is, is nothing short of astonishing. Despite the fact that there are four very different musicians and individuals on the stage, listening to the Emersons is like listening to one voice, indivisible and admirable.

André Previn
August 2001

The men of the Emerson String Quartet are amazing people. Generous, compassionate, humorous, artistic, and at times, mischievous.

In July of 1993, the construction of Harris Concert Hall at the Aspen Music Festival and School was about 95% complete. The opening was scheduled for August 20, 1993, but not one note of music had been played in the Hall. Needless to say, we were all quite anxious to know about the acoustics. On a Saturday afternoon, I asked the Emerson Quartet if they would mind coming a little early for their 4:00pm concert in the Music Tent so that we could hear some music in the new Hall. They readily agreed. They entered on stage in their concert dress, amid construction dust and materials, and sat down to begin to play. The first notes were totally inaudible, though, because the boys decided it would be pretty funny to play with their bows not touching the strings on their instruments! It was a wonderful tension-releasing moment, and after some much-needed laughter, they proceeded to play sublime Mozart, inaugurating a wonderful acoustic in our Harris Concert Hall with the most memorable playing imaginable.

Robert Harth
Artistic Director, Carnegie Hall

My musical and personal admiration for the members of the Emerson Quartet started in 1984, when I was asked to produce an album of romantic and impressionistic quartets with them. We had eight works to record in nine days, a daunting task which realistically required twice as much time.

To prepare for this budget-determined schedule, we all decided that I should attend the final rehearsals planned for the eight quartets so I could become familiar with their interpretations. In those rehearsals and the subsequent recording sessions, we quickly achieved a relaxed and interactive working relationship based on common musical values. Over the following years that relationship played a part in the creation of a large body of historic recordings.

Because of the Emerson's exceptional insight into a vast range of musical styles, their concerts and recordings give us authoritative performances of works spanning three centuries. During our collaboration the group recorded works of Ives, Barber, Rorem, Harbison, Schuller, Wernick, Meyer, Webern and Shostakovich. There were distinguished collaborations with Menahem Pressler in piano quartets and quintets of Schumann and Dvorak, and with David Shifrin in clarinet quintets of Mozart and Brahms.

All of this was capped by an award-winning recording of the complete quartets of Beethoven, which took two and a half years to complete. The sessions were notable for the Emerson's tireless quest for the exact character and mood of each movement of every quartet. Beethoven's metronome markings were considered and reconsidered. The spirit they indicated was never violated.

It was particularly in these great works that the individual personalities of Philip Setzer, Eugene Drucker, Lawrence Dutton and David Finckel made memorable contributions to the final performances. All fine string quartets strive to blend four players of individual character to produce a well-balanced musical unit. The Emerson Quartet is extraordinary for the variety of musical impulses that flow from its four virtuoso members. This produces performances notable for great poetry, emotional intensity and masterful rhythmic control. These qualities are all essential for great performances of Beethoven, and they are vividly present in these realizations of the music. I was happy to be there to urge them on.

Max Wilcox
Recording producer

About Risk Waters Group

Risk Waters Group is a specialist publishing and conference company headquartered in London, with offices in New York and Hong Kong. The company produces magazines, books, newsletters, web services, conferences and training courses on financial topics, especially risk management and financial technology.

Over the past six years, Risk Waters has sponsored many chamber music concerts at London's Wigmore Hall and South Bank Centre. In April 2001 it sponsored the Emerson String Quartet at the Wigmore Hall as part of the Hall's centenary celebrations; and in November 2001, Risk Waters was again the sponsor for all three of the Emerson's 25th anniversary concerts at the Queen Elizabeth Hall, part of the South Bank Centre.

Risk Waters also commissioned a chamber symphony, Cyclops (2000), from the American composer Charles Wuorinen, which was premiered at the QEH by the London Sinfonietta in May 2001.

Tragically, 16 people working for Risk Waters were killed in the World Trade Center terrorist attack of September 11, 2001, along with 71 other people attending a Risk Waters conference on the 106th floor of the WTC North Tower.

All proceeds from the sale of this book will go to the Risk Waters World Trade Center Appeal, UK, and the Risk Waters World Trade Center Foundation, Inc., set up to assist dependants of those killed on September 11.

Further information is available at www.riskwaters.com.